TABLE OF CONTENTS

Lesson Manual 2   111

br	Brad, brown*, broom*
cr	crack, crayons*, creep
dr	drag, dress, drop
fr	Fred, fruit, from*
gr	grab, Gram, grass, green
kr	Kris
pr	Prim, prize, prop
tr	tree, tries, trip, trunk

sk	skate, skin, skunk
sl	slam, slide, slimy*, slip, slither*
sm	smell, small*, smack

2

*sight words

Letter Lesson Instructions

Each letter lesson follows the same format as below. This page explains how to present each section of the letter lesson. This is also shown in the getting started video found under "training" at www.4weekstoread.com.

Note: Continuous praise and encouragement throughout the lesson is extremely important. Before beginning each lesson, read all the way through it.

LETTER NAME: This is the letter taught in the lesson. The upper-case (capital) and lower-case letters are shown. They are **not** in alphabetical order.

PRONUNCIATION: This tells you how to pronounce the letter as you teach it. When it is written like this–"a"–you say the letter name. When it is written like this–"aaaa"–you say the letter sound.

PREPARATION: Read through the lesson and listen to the letter song before you start. Included in your kit you will find a card of popout letter pieces, one for each letter. Find the one for the letter you are teaching. Pop it out. You will also need a pencil, and crayons for the child. Also look at the optional activity. If you choose to do it with your child, you may need to get the supplies ahead of time.

ALPHABET SONG: This song is to be sung every day at the beginning of the reading lesson. It is track #1. You can also download the music at www.4weekstoread.com by clicking on "music" at the top of the page. As you sing the song with your child, use the alphabet picture flash cards.

LETTER REVIEW: Review the letters and sounds you have just learned. These will be listed at the beginning of each lesson under "letter review." Use the blue letter flashcards. After every five letters learned there will be a review lesson and worksheet.

LETTER LESSONS: <u>Do three letter lessons a week. Each lesson consists of:</u>

1. **Introduction:** Use the blue letter flashcards to introduce the letter you are working on in the lesson. Show the letter to the child. Say the letter name and sound. Tell the child that there is a big letter and a little letter, and both letters make the same sound. You will work with the little letter.

2. **Story:** The story is to help the child remember the letter and its sound through association. Use the popout letter piece as a visual as you tell the story. **Emphasize the sound each time you say it.** The child keeps the letter piece after learning the letter and may want to keep these in a special place.

3. **Letter Song:** There is a song for each letter. It reinforces the sound the letter makes.

4. **Worksheet:** This is an activity that teaches the child what the letter looks like and how to write it. Show both upper- and lower-case letters, but only write the lower case. This activity also helps them hear the sound at the beginning of words. It is found in the child's workbook.

5. **Letter Song:** Listen to the letter song for the second time. This time sing along and, using the pictures and words on the back side of the letter lesson, point to the pictures as you repeat the words.

6. **Final Check:** As a final review of the letter and sound, show the blue letter flashcard one more time and ask the letter name and what it says. Then ask the child to say a word that starts with that sound. When the child responds correctly (give help if necessary), give praise and reward the child with a popout piece.

7. **Optional Activity:** These are suggested activities that reinforce the letter and sound. Have fun with these.

8. **Blending:** There are blending instructionson page 24. Blending is taught after the child has learned five of the letters. It teaches the child how to use the sounds they have learned in forming words. **They do not need to know all of the sounds before they can blend words and begin to read.** After blending has been taught, you will do a brief blending practice at the conclusion of each letter lesson.

BOOK PRESENTATION: Instructions for introducing the first book are on page 35. You have taught the first nine lessons. You have also taught blending on page 24. If the child is able to blend words, they are ready to begin reading books.

1. Always make sure the child can blend and read all of the new words in the book (a list is found at the beginning of each book) before you read the book.

2. Look at the book together and talk about the pictures.

3. Start at the beginning and have the child read the words. Be sure to sound out the words.

4. Give lots of praise and encouragement—help with the words if needed. Don't make them struggle.

5. Re-read the book until the child is quite fluent before moving on to the next book.

6. Read every day for 5-10 minutes. If at any time your child seems to be struggling, review previous lessons and re-read books that are easier. Then move on. There is no time pressure here. Make it a fun time together.

7. When you have completed the first 23 short-vowel books, re-read favorites until you have completed all of the letter lessons and two-vowel lessons. Then begin reading the two-vowel books.

Note: Make your reading time together fun and relaxed, but be in charge. Say to the child: "It's time to read now." Do not say, "Do you want to read now?" Make a set time and place to do reading each day and be consistent. If the child is not having a good day, shorten the time you work together. Use a lot of praise and rewards to motivate them. Help your child look forward to this special time with you.

Read through the lesson.

LETTER: Mm

PRONUNCIATION: "mmmm" as in mouse

PREPARATION: Punch out Morty Mouse from the popout letter piece cards.

ALPHABET SONG: Play track #1. Show the picture flash cards to the child as you sing along with the song.

Mm

LETTER LESSON:

Introduction: Show the child the blue letter card and say:	*This is the letter "m." There is a big "M" and a small "m." It says "mmmm." What letter is this?*
Point to the card and say "m" together. Ask the child:	*What does it say?*
Say "mmmm" together.	*Good.*

Story: Use the mouse to tell the story. Emphasize the letter sound.

Morty Munching Mouse loves to munch.
Munch, munch, munch. (mmmm—rub tummy)
Morty Munching Mouse munches macaroni.
Munch, munch, munch. (mmmm—rub tummy)
Morty Munching Mouse munches muffins.
Munch, munch, munch. (mmmm—rub tummy)
Morty Munching Mouse munches mushrooms.
Munch, munch, munch. (mmmm—rub tummy)
But most of all, Morty Munching Mouse loves to munch on
M&M's™—"mmmmmmmmm." (Rub tummy)
Munch, munch, munch. He just might munch on you!
(Pretend to munch on the child)

Letter Song: Play track #2. Sing along with the "m" song.

Worksheet: Found in the child's workbook on page 1. Show the child how to write the letter "m." Cross out the picture that **does not** start with the sound of "mmmm." Color the pictures that **do** start with the "mmmm" sound.

Letter Song: Sing the "m" song again. Repeat the chant of "m" words, pointing to the words and pictures on the back of this page as you chant.

Final Check: Ask the child: *What letter is this? What does it say? Can you tell me a word that starts with the sound of "mmmm"? Good! Now you may keep this little **M**orty **M**ouse. He will help you remember what "m" says.*

OPTIONAL ACTIVITY: Play the "M&M game." You go around the house looking for things that start with the sound of "mmmm." Each time the child either finds an object or just says an "m" word, he gets one M&M candy.

Mm

munching **muffins**

mushrooms **macaroni**

Read through the lesson.

LETTER: Aa

PRONUNCIATION: "aaaa" as in alligator

PREPARATION: Punch out Andrew Alligator from the popout letter piece cards.

LETTER REVIEW: Review the previous letter, Mm, using the blue letter cards.

ALPHABET SONG: Play track #1. Show the picture flash cards to the child as you sing along with the song.

Aa

LETTER LESSON:

Introduction: Show the child the blue letter card and say:	*This is the letter "a." There is a big "A" and a small "a." It says "aaaa." What letter is this?*
Point to the card and say "a" together. Ask the child:	*What does it say?*
Say "aaaa" together.	*Good.*
Story: Use the alligator to tell the story. Emphasize the letter sound.	*Andrew Alligator was sleeping. He felt so snuggly and warm in his blanket. Mother came to give him a bath. She took off his blanket, and all at once Andrew Alligator was so cold all he could do was cry, "aaaa—aaaa." "A" says "aaaa." Can you sound like Andrew Alligator?*

Letter Song: Play track #3. Sing along with the "a" song.

Worksheet: Found in the child's workbook on page 2. Show the child how to write the letter "a." Cross out the pictures that *do not* start with the sound of "aaaa." Color the pictures that *do* start with the "aaaa" sound.

Letter Song: Sing the "a" song again. Repeat the chant of "a" words, pointing to the words and pictures on the next page as you chant.

Final Check: Ask the child:

What letter is this? What does it say? Can you tell me a word that starts with the sound of "aaaa"? Good! Now you may keep this little Andrew Alligator. He will help you remember what "a" says."

OPTIONAL ACTIVITY: Feed the child an apple and remind them that apple starts with the "aaaa" sound. Praise, praise, praise.

Aa

Point to these words as you sing the letter song.

apple

antlers

ant

alligator

Read through the lesson.

LETTER: Pp

PRONUNCIATION: "pppp" as in pig

PREPARATION: Punch out Parley the pink pig from the popout letter piece cards.

LETTER REVIEW: Review the previous letters Mm and Aa.

ALPHABET SONG: Play track #1. Show the picture flash cards to the child as you sing along with the song.

Pp

LETTER LESSON:

Introduction: Show the child the blue letter card and say:	*This is the letter "p." There is a big "P" and a small "p." It says "pppp." What letter is this?*
Point to the card and say "p" together. Ask the child:	*What does it say?*
Say "pppp" together.	*Good!*
Story: Use the pig to tell the story. Emphasize the letter sound.	*Parley the pink pig plays the piano. He plinks and he plunks the pretty tunes. People pay attention to his playing partly because he is a pig—a pink pig—and it is not very often you see a pink pig named Parley who can play the piano.*

Letter Song: Play track #4. Sing along with the "p" song.

Worksheet: Found in the child's workbook on page 3. Show the child how to write the letter "p." Cross out the pictures that *do not* start with the sound of "pppp." Color the pictures that *do* start with the "pppp" sound.

Letter Song: Sing the "p" song again. Repeat the chant of "p" words, pointing to the words and pictures on the next page as you chant.

Final Check: Ask the child:

What letter is this? What does it say? Can you tell me a word that starts with the sound of "pppp"? Good! Now you may keep this little pig. It will help you remember what "p" says.

OPTIONAL ACTIVITY: Find things around the house that start with the "pppp" sound. Make popcorn and listen to the popping sound. Make the sound with the pop.

Pp

Point to these words as you sing the letter song.

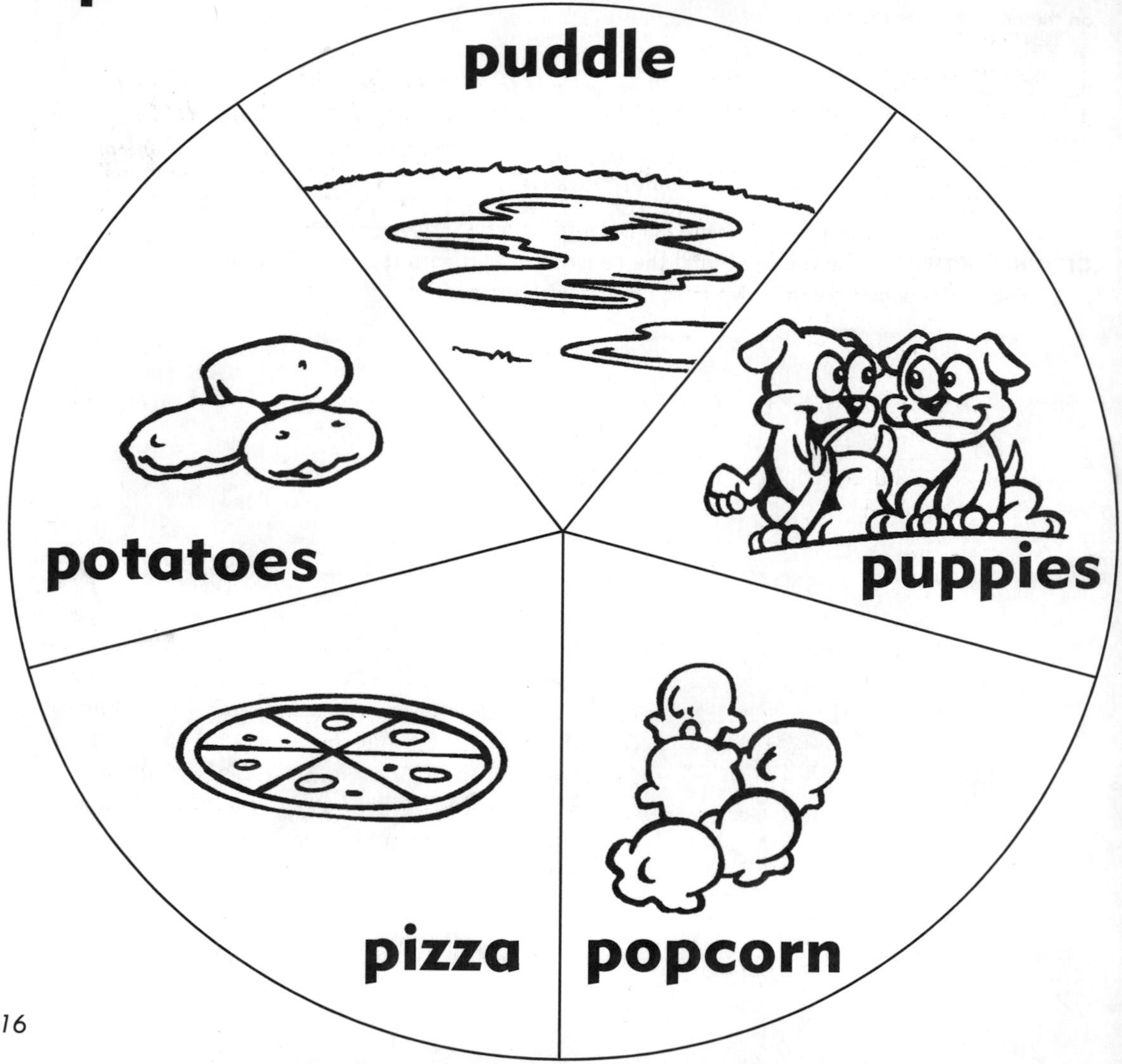

puddle

potatoes

puppies

pizza

popcorn

Read through the lesson.

LETTER: Ss

PRONUNCIATION: "ssss" as in snake

PREPARATION: Punch out Sammy the Snake from the popout letter piece cards.

LETTER REVIEW: Review the previous letters Mm, Aa, and Pp using blue letter cards.

ALPHABET SONG: Play track #1. Show the picture flash cards to the child as you sing along with the song.

LETTER LESSON:

Introduction: Show the child the blue letter card and say:	*This is the letter "s." There is a big "S" and a small "s." It says "ssss." What letter is this?*
Point to the card and say "s" together. Ask the child:	*What does it say?*
Say "ssss" together.	*Good!*
Story: Use the snake to tell the story. Emphasize the letter sound.	*My name is Sammy the Snake. I love spots and I love stripes too. My sister and I sleep under the stairs at the school. I love to slip and slither around on my snake skin in the sand. Sometimes I slide with other slippery snakes. I surprise everyone with a sound like "ssss." I eat sandwiches, salad, and sausages. My favorite numbers are six and seven. I am a special snake who loves to sing solos. Sometimes I am silly. "SSSSSSSSSSSS" (laughing through teeth).*

Letter Song: Play track #5. Sing along with the "s" song.

Worksheet: Found in the child's workbook on page 4. Show the child how to write the letter "s." Cross out the pictures that *do not* start with the sound of "ssss." Color the pictures that *do* start with the "ssss" sound.

Letter Song: Sing the "s" song again. Repeat the chant of "s" words, pointing to the words and pictures on the next page as you chant.

Final Check: Ask the child:

What letter is this? What does it say? Can you tell me a word that starts with the sound of "ssss"? Good! Now you may keep this little snake. He will help you remember what "s" says.

OPTIONAL ACTIVITY: Let the child play with the snake finding things that start with "ssss." Praise, praise, and praise.

Ss

slip   **slide**

sand   **snake**

Read through the lesson.

LETTER: Tt

PRONUNCIATION: "tttt" as in turtle

PREPARATION: Punch out Timothy Turtle from the popout letter piece cards.

LETTER REVIEW: Review the previous letters Mm, Aa, Pp, and Ss.

ALPHABET SONG: Play track #1. Show the picture flash cards to the child as you sing along with the song.

Tt

LETTER LESSON:

Introduction: Show the child the blue letter card and say:	*This is the letter "t." There is a big "T" and a small "t." It says "tttt." What letter is this?*
Point to the card and say "t" together. Ask the child:	*What does it say?*
Say "tttt" together.	*Good!*
Story: Use the turtle to tell the story. Emphasize the letter sound.	*Tiny Timothy Turtle was terribly tardy. Hurry Timothy! Try to hurry so you can be on time. But Timothy had trouble trying to hurry. Try as he might, all he could do was twist, twirl, and tumble over his tiny toes. "Timothy, now is not the time for turtle tricks!"*

Letter Song: Play track #6. Sing along with the "t" song.

Worksheet: Found in the child's workbook on page 5. Show the child how to write the letter "t." Cross out the pictures that *do not* start with the sound of "tttt." Color the pictures that *do* start with the "tttt" sound.

Letter Song: Sing the "t" song again. Repeat the chant of "t" words, pointing to the words and pictures on the next of this page as you chant.

Final Check: Ask the child:

What letter is this? What does it say? Can you tell me a word that starts with the sound of "tttt"? Good! Now you may keep this little turtle. He will help you remember what "t" says.

OPTIONAL ACTIVITY: Find things around the house that start with the "tttt" sound. Write the name of these things on a piece of paper underlining the letter "t." Put this up somewhere that the child can easily see.

Tt

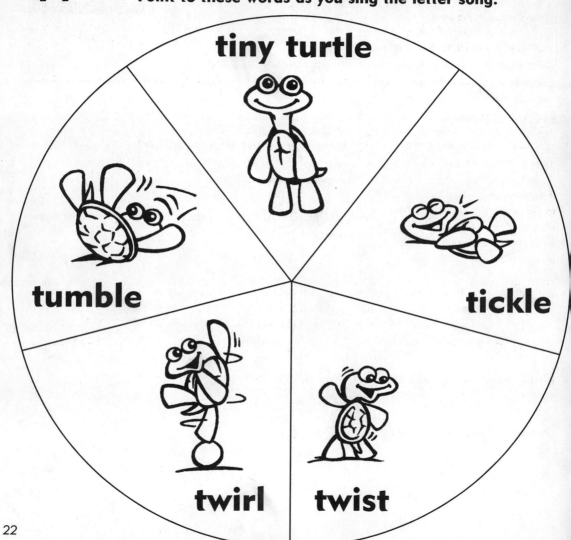

tiny turtle

tumble

tickle

twirl

twist

22

Read through the lesson.

LETTERS TO REVIEW: Mm, Aa, Pp, Ss, and Tt.
PREPARATION: Find the letters in the picture flash cards.

REVIEW LESSON:

Introduction: Show the picture flash cards, one letter at a time. Ask the child:

What letter is this? What does it say?

If they are unable to remember, refer to the picture on the card and the story used to teach the letter. Say the letter name and the sound it makes several times.

Worksheet: Show the child the worksheet found in the child's workbook on page 6. Tell them the names of the things pictured, emphasizing the beginning sound. Show them how to match the letter with the picture of the same beginning sound. Draw a line between them with your finger. Then have the child draw the lines with a crayon and color the picture.

Final Check: Show each card again and ask:

What letter is this? What does it say?

Give lots of positive praise and encouragement.

Read through the lesson.

PREPARATION: Find the blue letter cards m, a, p, s, and t.

WATCH THE BLENDING INSTRUCTIONS VIDEO AT
WWW.4WEEKSTOREAD.COM UNDER THE TRAINING TAB.

BLENDING INSTRUCTIONS:

Review the letters and sounds—m, a, p, s, t—by using the blue letter cards. For each letter, ask the child:

What letter is this? What does it say?

If they have trouble with a letter, go back and review that letter lesson.

Ask the child:

Did you know these sounds can be put together to make a word? When you know words you can read!

Say to the child:

I have a little motor in my mouth. When I turn it on, it will say a sound—"mmmm." If I leave my motor running, it will make the sound last longer—"mmmmmmm." Then I can put it with other sounds. Listen.

What does this letter say? "aaaa" (blue letter card)
What does this letter say? "mmmm" (blue letter card)

(Run finger under the letters.)

Now listen while I make my mouth motor stay on. "aaaaammmm"

Let's do it again!   *"aaaammm"*

Now faster!   *"aaamm"*

Listen for the word! "am"

Great! Good job!

Let's do another word!
    What does this letter say?   "mmmm"
    What does this letter say?   "aaaa"
    What does this letter say?   " tttt"

Now listen while I make my mouth motor stay on.
"mmmaaattt"

Do it again, faster and faster until the child gets it (mat). Repeat this process with other words—as, at, sam, sat, and pam. This is the way you will teach blending at the end of each lesson.

Read through the lesson.

LETTER: Bb

PRONUNCIATION: "bbbb" as in bear

PREPARATION: Punch out Baby Bear from the popout letter piece cards.

LETTER REVIEW: Review the previous letters Mm, Aa, Pp, Ss, and Tt.

ALPHABET SONG: Play track #1. Show the picture flash cards to the child as you sing along with the song.

Bb

LETTER LESSON:

Introduction: Show the child the blue letter card and say:	*This is the letter "b." There is a big "B" and a small "b." It says "bbbb." What letter is this?*
Point to the card and say "b" together. Ask the child:	*What does it say?*
Say "bbbb" together.	*Good!*
Story: Use the bear to tell the story. Emphasize the letter sound.	*Baby Bear was bouncing his big ball. Every time he bounced his ball he heard a special sound—b b b b. "That is my favorite sound," said Baby Bear—b b b b! He bounced the ball. He batted the ball. He balanced the ball. "Boy! I love to play ball!" "bbbb."*

Letter Song: Play track #7. Sing along with the "b" song.

Worksheet: Found in the child's workbook on page 7. Show the child how to write the letter "b." Cross out the pictures that *do not* start with the sound of "bbbb." Color the pictures that *do* start with the "bbbb" sound.

Letter Song: Sing the "b" song again. Repeat the chant of "b" words, pointing to the words and pictures on the back of this page as you chant.

Final Check: Ask the child: *"What letter is this? What does it say? Can you tell me a word that starts with the sound of "bbbb"? Good! Now you may keep this little bear. He will help you remember what "b" says."*

OPTIONAL ACTIVITY: Let the child bounce a ball and make the "bbbb" sound. Find things around the house that start with the "bbbb" sound. If the child has a favorite teddy bear, let him name it something starting with a "b."

BLENDING: Blend the previous letters together to form words—bat, bam, tab, mat, pat, Sam, and Pam.

Bb

baby   **bear**

bouncing   **ball**

Read through the lesson.

LETTER: Hh

PRONUNCIATION: "hhhh" as in horse

PREPARATION: Punch out Henrietta Horse from the popout letter piece cards.

LETTER REVIEW: Review the previous letters Mm, Aa, Pp, Ss, Tt, and Bb.

ALPHABET SONG: Play track #1. Show the picture flash cards to the child as you sing along with the song.

Hh

LETTER LESSON:

Introduction: Show the child the blue letter card and say:	*This is the letter "h." There is a big "H" and a small "h." It says "hhhh." What letter is this?*
Point to the card and say "h" together. Ask the child:	*What does it say?*
Say "hhhh" together.	*Good!*

Story: Use the horse to tell the story. Emphasize the letter sound.	*Once there was a **h**appy **h**orse named **H**enrietta. She **h**ad pretty golden **h**air and walked with **h**er **h**ead **h**eld **h**igh. She would **h**oller to the **h**ogs, "**H**ello." They only laughed, "**h**a, **h**a, **h**a." She was so sad she wanted to **h**ide in a **h**ole. Then one day a **h**ummingbird **h**ummed in **H**enrietta's ear, "put on your **h**appy **h**at, and they will no longer laugh "**h**a, **h**a, **h**a." So **H**enrietta **H**orse did as she was told. She put on **h**er **h**appy **h**at, and she was **h**appy ever after because no one laughed at her. Everyone was just **h**appy.*

Letter Song: Play track #8. Sing along with the "h" song.

Worksheet: Found in the child's workbook on page 8. Show the child how to write the letter "h." Cross out the pictures that *do not* start with the sound of "hhhh." Color the pictures that *do* start with the "hhhh" sound.

Letter Song: Sing the "h" song again. Repeat the chant of "h" words, pointing to the words and pictures on the next page as you chant.

Final Check: Ask the child:

What letter is this? What does it say? Can you tell me a word that starts with the sound of "hhhh"? Good! Now you may keep this little horse. It will help you remember what "h" says.

OPTIONAL ACTIVITY: Say "h" words while hanging a tissue loose in front of your mouth. It will flutter if the sound is correct. (Give the child a tissue to hold in front of his mouth as he says "hhhh." The tissue should flutter if the child is saying it correctly.)

BLENDING: Blend the previous letters together to form words—hat, ham, bat, and sat.

Hh

Point to these words as you sing the letter song.

head

horse

hair

hummingbird

hat

Read through the lesson.

LETTER: Gg

PRONUNCIATION: "gggg" as in ghost

PREPARATION: Punch out Goofy Ghost from the popout letter piece cards.

LETTER REVIEW: Review the previous letters Hh, Bb, and Tt.

ALPHABET SONG: Play track #1. Show the picture flash cards to the child as you sing along with the song.

LETTER LESSON:

Introduction: Show the child the blue letter card and say:	*This is the letter "g." There is a big "G" and a small "g." It says "gggg." What letter is this?*
Point to the card and say "g" together. Ask the child:	*What does it say?*
Say "gggg" together.	*Good!*
Story: Use the ghost to tell the story. Read it in a scary voice. Emphasize the letter sound.	*One night **G**oofy **G**host was **g**oing out to **g**ather his friends to **g**o **g**hosting. All at once he **g**asped. A **g**rating noise scared him. "**G-G-G-g**o away!" Cried **G**oofy. "I'm **G-G-G**-**G**oofy **G-G-G-G**host. You can't scare me." But it was only the creaky **g**arden **g**ate. Next he saw a **g**reat, **g**lowing ball, It was so scary. "**G-G-G-G**o away!" Cried **G**oofy. "I'm **G**-**G-G-G**oofy **G**host. You can't scare me." But it was only a **g**littering porch light. "Oh my **g**oodness!" **G**runted **G**oofy, "what do you **g**uess is **g**rowing in the **g**arbage can? It looks **g**reen and **g**ooey, and **g**ross! **G-G-G-G**o away!" Cried **G**oofy. "I'm **G-G-G**-**G**oofy **G**host. You can't scare me!" "I can't **g**uess what it is," said **G**oofy. "Is it a **g**oblin? Is it a **g**reat **g**rowling monster?" " **GOTCHA!!!!!!!**"*

Letter Song: Play track #9. Sing along with the "g" song.

Worksheet: Found in the child's workbook on page 9. Show the child how to write the letter "g." Cross out the pictures that *do not* start with the sound of "gggg." Color the pictures that *do* start with the "gggg" sound.

Letter Song: Sing the "g" song again. Repeat the chant of "g" words, pointing to the words and pictures on the next page as you chant.

Final Check: Ask the child:

What letter is this? What does it say? Can you tell me a word that starts with the sound of "gggg"? Good! Now you may keep this little ghost. It will help you remember what "g" says.

OPTIONAL ACTIVITY: Creep around the house looking for "g" words. Play like it's scary.

BLENDING: Blend the previous letters together to form words—gas, gab, sag, tag, and bag.

Gg

Point to these words as you sing the letter song.

ghost

girl

gift

gate

If the child has grasped the concept of blending sounds to make words, they are now ready to read Book 1. If they are not blending words, don't be frustrated, but continue learning and reviewing the letters and sounds and practice blending until they can do it. Then start Book 1.

BOOK PRESENTATION:

As soon as the child is able to blend sounds and make words, they are ready to begin reading books. Review all the letters learned—m, a, p, s, t, b, h, and g.

1. Introduce and help sound out all the new words in the book before you begin reading. A list of the words is found inside the front cover of each book. As you progress into the books there will be a few sight words to learn. These are words that cannot be sounded out. They are listed separately at the beginning of each book. Just tell the child what these words are. With practice, the child will learn these words.

2. Look at the book together and talk about the pictures.

3. Start at the beginning and have the child read the words by sounding them out.

4. Give lots of praise and encouragement—help with the words if needed. Don't make them struggle.

5. Re-read the book until the child is quite fluent before moving on to the next book.

6. Read every day for 5-10 minutes.

7. Read through the blue books, re-reading your favorites as you continue to progress through the letter lessons. Once you have completed the 2-vowel lessons(Lessons 33-41) you can begin reading the red books.

Read through the lesson.

LETTER: Dd

PRONUNCIATION: "dddd" as in dinosaur

PREPERATION: Punch out the dinosaur from the popout letter piece card. Make up the "dinosaur detector" found on page 39 of your instruction manual. Hide the dinosaur in the house to be found during the lesson. You will go on a dinosaur hunt around your house to find "d" objects. Identify what you might find—door, desk, daddy, doll, dog, etc. Use the detector to guide you to these things. When you find a "d" object, make a fast "dddd" sound.

LETTER REVIEW: Review the previous letters—Bb, Hh, and Gg—using blue letter cards.

ALPHABET SONG: Play track #1. Show the picture flash cards to the child as you sing along with the song.

LETTER LESSON:

Introduction: Show the child the blue letter card and say:	*This is the letter "d." There is a big "D" and a small "d." It says "dddd." What letter is this?*
Point to the card and say "d" together. Ask the child:	*What does it say?*
Say "dddd" together.	*Good!*
Story: Use the dinosaur detector to tell the story. Emphasize the letter sound.	***Dr. D**udley and his **d**og **D**ufus are hunting for **d**inosaurs. They are using a special **d**inosaur **d**etector. It says "dddd" when it finds something that starts with a "d." (Look around the house for "d" objects. The detector sounds slow when looking for something that starts with a "d", and fast when sitting on a "d" object. Finally the last object found is a dinosaur.) **Dr. D**udley has found a **d**inosaur—a **d**arling, **d**ancing **d**inosaur!*

Letter Song: Play track #10. Sing along with the "d" song.

Worksheet: Found in the child's workbook on page 10. Show the child how to write the letter "d." Cross out the pictures that *do not* start with the sound of "dddd." Color the pictures that *do* start with the "dddd" sound.

Letter Song: Sing the "d" song again. Repeat the chant of "d" words, pointing to the words and pictures on the next page as you chant.

Final Check: Ask the child:

What letter is this? What does it say? Can you tell me a word that starts with the sound of "dddd"? Good! Now you may keep this little dinosaur. He will help you remember what "d" says.

OPTIONAL ACTIVITY: Find other things around the house that start with "d" using the detector. Examples: door, desk, dish, doll, dog.

BLENDING: Blend the previous letters together to form words—dad, sad, mad, had, and bad.

Dd

Point to these words as you sing the letter song.

dolphin

doughnut

dog

dinosaur

Dinosaur Detector

Directions:
1. Cut out the arrow and the circle.
2. Place the arrow on the top of the circle and attach with a brad.

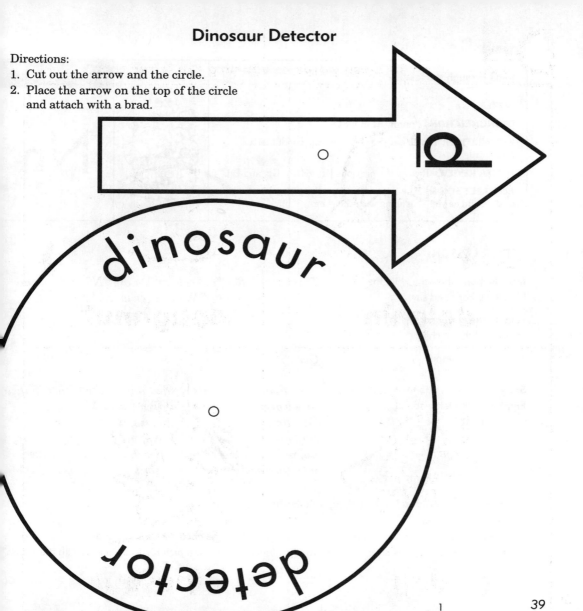

1

Read through the lesson.

LETTER: Nn

PRONUNCIATION: "nnnn" as in nest

PREPARATION: Punch out the nest from the popout letter piece cards.

LETTER REVIEW: Review the previous letters Hh, Gg, and Dd.

ALPHABET SONG: Play track #1. Show the picture flash cards to the child as you sing along with the song.

Nn

LETTER LESSON:

Introduction: Show the child the blue letter card and say:	*This is the letter "n." There is a big "N" and a small "n." It says "nnnn." What letter is this?*
Point to the card and say "n" together. Ask the child:	*What does it say?*
Say "nnnn" together.	*Good!*
Story: Use the nest to tell the story. Emphasize the letter sound.	*Nine noisy, little birds nestled next to each other in their nice warm nest. "Now, children," said Mommy Bird, "It's time to fly." "No, no, no, no, no, no, no, no, no," said the nine, noisy birds, "No, no, no, no, no, no, no, no, no! Never, never, never, never, never, never, never, never, never!" "Come now," said Mommy, "Let's fly!"*

Letter Song: Play track #11. Sing along with the "n" song.

Worksheet: Found in the child's workbook on page 11. Show the child how to write the letter "n." Cross out the pictures that *do not* start with the sound of "nnnn." Color the pictures that *do* start with the "nnnn" sound.

Letter Song: Sing the "n" song again. Repeat the chant of "n" words, pointing to the words and pictures on the next page as you chant.

Final Check: Ask the child:

What letter is this? What does it say? Can you tell me a word that starts with the sound of "nnnn"? Good! Now you may keep this little nest. It will help you remember what "n" says.

OPTIONAL ACTIVITY: Find things around the house that start with the "nnnn" sound.

BLENDING: Blend the previous letters together to form words—man, tan, nap, ant, and pan.

Nn

Point to these words as you sing the letter song.

nose

nails

nest

nut

Read through the lesson.

LETTERS TO REVIEW: Bb, Hh, Gg, Dd, and Nn.

PREPARATION: Find the letters in the picture flash cards.

REVIEW LESSON:

Introduction: Show the picture flash cards, one letter at a time. Ask the child:

What letter is this? What does it say?

If they are unable to remember, refer to the picture on the card and the story used to teach the letter. Say the letter name and the sound it makes several times.

Worksheet: Show the child the worksheet found in the child's workbook on page 12. Tell them the names of the things pictured, emphasizing the beginning sound. Show them how to match the letter with the picture of the same beginning sound. Draw a line between them with your finger. Then have the child draw the lines with a crayon and color the picture.

Final Check: Show each card again and ask:

What letter is this? What does it say?

Give lots of positive praise and encouragement.

LETTER: Rr

PRONUNCIATION: "rrrr" as in rabbit

PREPARATION: Punch out Robby Rabbit from the popout letter piece cards.

LETTER REVIEW: Review the previous letters Gg, Dd, and Nn.

ALPHABET SONG: Play track #1. Show the picture flash cards to the child as you sing along with the song.

Rr

LETTER LESSON:

Introduction: Show the child the blue letter card and say:	*This is the letter "r." There is a big "R" and a small "r." It says "rrrr." What letter is this?*
Point to the card and say "r" together. Ask the child:	*What does it say?*
Say "rrrr" together.	*Good!*
Story: Use the rabbit to tell the story. Emphasize the letter sound.	*Robby Rabbit loves to race. He is off like a rocket, running rapidly down the road. He runs over the river and right up the ridge. Oh! Be careful! Robby Rabbit trips and rolls right into a rock! But he remembers not to rest, and he races to the red rope at the finish line. Robby Rabbit wins!*

Letter Song: Play track #12. Sing along with the "r" song.

Worksheet: Found in the child's workbook on page 13. Show the child how to write the letter "r." Cross out the pictures that *do not* start with the sound of "rrrr." Color the pictures that *do* start with the "rrrr" sound.

Letter Song: Sing the "r" song again. Repeat the chant of "r" words, pointing to the words and pictures on the next page as you chant.

Final Check: Ask the child:

What letter is this? What does it say? Can you tell me a word that starts with the sound of "rrrr?" Good! Now you may keep this little rabbit. He will help you remember what "r" says.

OPTIONAL ACTIVITY: Find things around the house that start with the "rrrr" sound.

BLENDING: Blend the previous letters together to form words—rat, ram, rad, ran, and rag.

Rr

rabbit

rocket

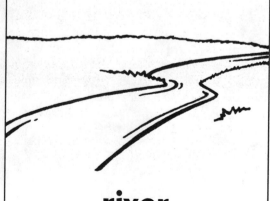

river

rock and roll

46

Read through the lesson.

LETTER: Ll

PRONUNCIATION: "llll" as in lamb

PREPARATION: Punch out Lilly Lamb from the popout letter piece cards.

LETTER REVIEW: Review the previous letters Dd, Nn, and Rr.

ALPHABET SONG: Play track #1. Show the picture flash cards to the child as you sing along with the song.

LETTER LESSON:

Introduction: Show the child the blue letter card and say:	*This is the letter "l." There is a big "L" and a small "l." It says "llll." What letter is this?*
Point to the card and say "l" together. Ask the child:	*What does it say?*
Say "llll" together.	*Good!*
Story: Use the lamb to tell the story. Emphasize the letter sound.	*Lovely Lilly Lamb was on her way to the library. She was licking her large, lemon-lime lollipop. Suddenly the lollipop latched onto her lovely lips. Larry was lurking at the library door. "Look!" He said, laughing at Lilly, "There is a lollipop latched to her lips! You can't go into the library like that!" Lilly licked and licked that luscious lollipop until it was all gone. It is lucky because Lilly loved to go to the library.*

Letter Song: Play track #13. Sing along with the "l" song.

Worksheet: Found in the child's workbook on page 14. Show the child how to write the letter "l." Cross out the pictures that *do not* start with the sound of "llll." Color the pictures that *do* start with the "llll" sound.

Letter Song: Sing the "l" song again. Repeat the chant of "l" words, pointing to the words and pictures on the next page as you chant.

Final Check: Ask the child:

What letter is this? What does it say? Can you tell me a word that starts with the sound of "llll"? Good! Now you may keep this little lamb. It will help you remember what "l" says.

OPTIONAL ACTIVITY: Find things around the house that start with "l." Give the child a lollipop to lick.

BLENDING: Blend the previous letters together to form words—lad, lag, lab, pal, and gal.

Ll

lion

lamp

leaf

lamb

49

Read through the lesson.

LETTER: Cc

PRONUNCIATION: "cccc" as in caterpillar

PREPARATION: Punch out Cameron Caterpillar from the popout letter piece cards.

LETTER REVIEW: Review previous letters Nn, Rr, and Ll using the blue letter cards.

ALPHABET SONG: Play track #1. Show the picture flash cards to the child as you sing along with the song.

Cc

LETTER LESSON:

Introduction: Show the child the blue letter card and say:	*This is the letter "c." There is a big "C" and a small "c." It says "cccc." What letter is this?*
Point to the card and say "c" together. Ask the child:	*What does it say?*
Say "cccc" together.	*Good!*
Story: Use the caterpillar to tell the story. Emphasize the letter sound.	*Connie the cute caterpillar crawled up the wall. "Come on you guys," she said to her cousins. "Can't you hurry faster?" "Course not," said Cameron. "Cause we are creepy crawly caterpillars."*

Letter Song: Play track #14. Sing along with the "c" song.

Worksheet: Found in the child's workbook on page 15. Show the child how to write the letter "c." Cross out the pictures that *do not* start with the sound of "cccc." Color the pictures that *do* start with the "cccc" sound.

Letter Song: Sing the "c" song again. Repeat the chant of "c" words, pointing to the words and pictures on the next page as you chant.

Final Check: Ask the child:

What letter is this? What does it say? Can you tell me a word that starts with the sound of "cccc"? Good! Now you may keep this little Cameron Caterpillar. He will help you remember what "c" says.

OPTIONAL ACTIVITY: Give the child some candy and remind them that candy starts with "c." Find things around the house that start with "cccc" sound.

BLENDING: Blend the previous letters together to form words—cat, cap, can, and cab.

Cc

cat

card

corn

candy cane

Read through the lesson.

LETTER: Jj

PRONUNCIATION: "jjjj" as in jack in the box

TEACHING AID: Punch out Jolly Jack in the Box from the popout letter piece cards.

LETTER REVIEW: Review the previous letters Rr, Ll, and Cc.

ALPHABET SONG: Play track #1. Show the picture flash cards to the child as you sing along with the song.

Jj

LETTER LESSON:

Introduction: Show the child the blue letter card and say:	*This is the letter "j." There is a big "J" and a small "j." It says "jjjj." What letter is this?*
Point to the card and say "j" together. Ask the child:	*What does it say?*
Say "jjjj" together.	*Good!*
Story: Use the jack in the box to tell the story. Emphasize the letter sound.	*Jolly Jack-in-the-Box jumped up to see the jar of jelly beans. Just how many do you think he saw? It was hard to tell because those jelly beans were jumping all over the place. Some jelly beans even jumped out of the jar. What a joke! Jolly Jack-in-the-Box just laughed his jolly laugh.*

Letter Song: Play track #15. Sing along with the "j" song.

Worksheet: Found in the child's workbook on page 16. Show the child how to write the letter "j." Cross out the pictures that *do not* start with the sound of "jjjj." Color the pictures that *do* start with the "jjjj" sound.

Letter Song: Sing the "j" song again. Repeat the chant of "j" words, pointing to the words and pictures on the next page as you chant.

Final Check: Ask the child:

What letter is this? What does it say? Can you tell me a word that starts with the sound of "jjjj"? Good! Now you may keep this little Jack-in-the-Box. It will help you remember what "j" says.

OPTIONAL ACTIVITY: Put some jelly beans in a jar and use to illustrate the story. The child gets to eat one jelly bean for each "j" word he can say.

BLENDING: Blend the previous letters together to form words— jam, Jan, and jab.

Jj

Point to these words as you sing the letter song.

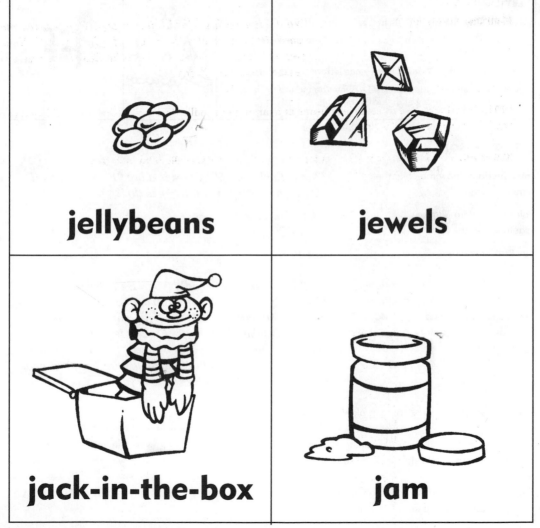

jellybeans	**jewels**
jack-in-the-box	**jam**

55

Read through the lesson.

LETTER: Ff

PRONUNCIATION: "ffff" as in frog

PREPARATION: Punch out Friendly Frog from the popout letter piece cards.

LETTER REVIEW: Review the previous letters Ll, Cc, and Jj.

ALPHABET SONG: Play track #1. Show the picture flash cards to the child as you sing along. with the song.

LETTER LESSON:

Introduction: Show the child the blue letter card and say:	*This is the letter "f." There is a big "F" and a small "f." It says "ffff." What letter is this?*
Point to the card and say "f" together. Ask the child:	*What does it say?*
Say "ffff" together.	*Good!*
Story: Use the frog to tell the story. Emphasize the letter sound. On the next page you will find the lily pads to be used with the story.	*Freddy is a funny, friendly frog. He is trying to find his family. Father says, "Jump only on the "f" word lily pads or you will fall into the frightening, foaming pond." Can you help him? Freddy is not as smart as you. He cannot tell which ones are "f" words. (Have the child tell which ones the frog should land on.) If he is wrong—Help! Help! He starts to fall.*

Letter Song: Play track #16. Sing along with the "f" song.

Worksheet: Found in the child's workbook on page 17. Show the child how to write the letter "f." Cross out the pictures that *do not* start with the sound of "ffff." Color the pictures that *do* start with the "ffff" sound.

Letter Song: Sing the "f" song again. Repeat the chant of "f" words, pointing to the words and pictures on the next page as you chant.

Ff

Point to these words as you sing the letter song.

frog

fish

foot

fork

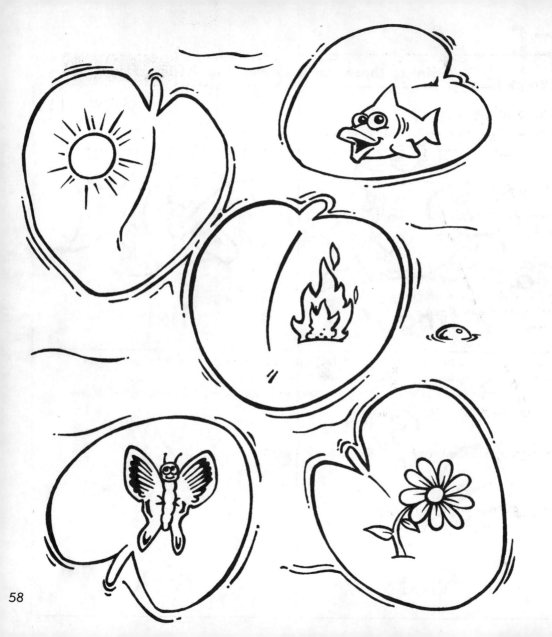

Read through the lesson.

LETTERS TO REVIEW: Rr, Ll, Cc, Jj, and Ff.

PREPARATION: Find the letters in the picture flash cards.

REVIEW LESSON:

Introduction: Show the picture flash cards, one letter at a time. Ask the child:

What letter is this? What does it say?

If they are unable to remember, refer to the picture on the card and the story used to teach the letter. Say the letter name and the sound it makes several times.

Worksheet: Show the child the worksheet found in the child's workbook on page 18. Tell them the names of the things pictured, emphasizing the beginning sound. Show them how to match the letter with the picture of the same beginning sound. Draw a line between them with your finger. Then have the child draw the lines with a crayon and color the picture.

Final Check: Show each card again and ask:

What letter is this? What does it say?

Give lots of positive praise and encouragement.

LETTER: Oo

PRONUNCIATION: "oooo" as in octopus

PREPARATION: Punch out Ollie Octopus from the popout letter piece cards.

LETTER REVIEW: Review the previous letters Cc, Jj, and Ff.

ALPHABET SONG: Play track #1. Show the picture flash cards to the child as you sing along with the song.

LETTER LESSON:

Introduction: Show the child the blue letter card and say:	*This is the letter "o." There is a big "O" and a small "o." It says "oooo." What letter is this?*
Point to the card and say "o" together. Ask the child:	*What does it say?*
Say "oooo" together.	*Good!*
Story: Use the octopus to tell the story. Emphasize the letter sound.	*Ollie Octopus sat on a rock. He was stuck! His legs were not working. They just hung there—straight as could be. "Help!" He hollered, "I cannot get off. How can I make my legs work? What are the magic words that will do it?" Maybe the "o" words that start with the "oooo" sound will do it. Let's try. "Octopus—oh yes, one leg is working. Olive—that feels so good. Office, Oscar, off, opposite, on, ostrich—Finally, all my legs are working!"*

Letter Song: Play track #17. Sing along with the "o" song.

Worksheet: Found in the child's workbook on page 19. Show the child how to write the letter "o." Cross out the pictures that *do not* start with the sound of "oooo." Color the pictures that *do* start with the "oooo" sound.

Letter Song: Sing the "o" song again. Repeat the chant of "o" words, pointing to the words and pictures on the next page as you chant.

Final Check: Ask the child:

What letter is this? What does it say? Can you tell me a word that starts with the sound of "oooo"? Good! Now you may keep this little octopus. It will help you remember what "o" says.

OPTIONAL ACTIVITY: Make the child an omelette to eat.

BLENDING: Blend the previous letters together to form words—hop, top, pop, mop, nod, rod, got, not, and dot.

Oo

Point to these words as you sing the letter song.

olive

ostrich

officer

octopus

Read through the lesson.

LETTER: Xx

PRONUNCIATION: "ks" as in box. (We are learning the "x" sound at the end of words rather than the beginning. This is what they need to do to begin reading.)

PREPARATION: Punch out Max the Fox from the popout letter piece card. Make a little treasure box. Fill with something you have at home that the child enjoys—game, story book, treat, video, etc. Make a trail of x's out of tape on the floor leading to the treasure box.

LETTER REVIEW: Review the previous letters Jj, Ff, and Oo.

ALPHABET SONG: Play track #1. Show the picture flash cards to the child as you sing along with the song.

LETTER LESSON:

Introduction: Show the child the blue letter card and say:	*This is the letter "x." There is a big "X" and a small "x." It says "xxxx." What letter is this?*
Point to the card and say "x" together. Ask the child:	*What does it say?*
Say "xxxx" together.	*Good!*
Story: Use the fox to tell the story. Emphasize the letter sound.	*Max the fox is searching for a treasure box. He needs our help to find it. Follow the X's and discover what the treasure is. (As you step on each X, say the sound of "x"). Find the treasure box and open it, but wait to do the activity until after the lesson.*

Letter Song: Play track #18. Sing along with the "x" song.

Worksheet: Found in the child's workbook on page 20. Show the child how to write the letter "x." Cross out the pictures that *do not* end with the sound of "xxxx." Color the pictures that *do* end with the "xxxx" sound.

Letter Song: Sing the "x" song again. Repeat the chant of "x" words, pointing to the words and pictures on the next page as you chant.

Final Check: Ask the child:

What letter is this? What does it say? Can you tell me a word that ends with the sound of "xxxx"? Good! Now you may keep this little fox. It will help you remember what "x" says.

OPTIONAL ACTIVITY: Do the activity you have chosen to put in the treasure box.

BLENDING: Blend the previous letters together to form words—tax, max, box, fox, and ax.

Xx

Point to these words as you sing the letter song.

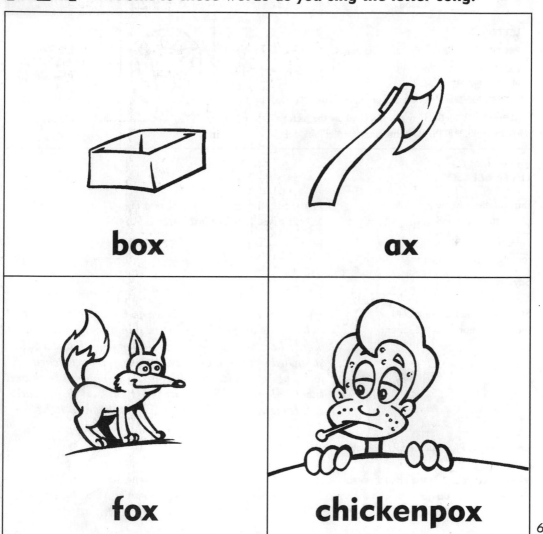

box

ax

fox

chickenpox

Read through the lesson.

LETTER: Ii

PRONUNCIATION: "iiii" as in iguana.

PREPARATION: Punch out Iggy Iguana from the popout letter piece cards.

LETTER REVIEW: Review the previous letters Xx, Oo, and Ll.

ALPHABET SONG: Play track #1. Show the picture flash cards to the child as you sing along with the song.

Ii

LETTER LESSON:

Introduction: Show the child the blue letter card and say:	*This is the letter "i." There is a big "I" and a small "i." It says "iiii". What letter is this?*
Point to the card and say "i" together. Ask the child:	*What does it say?*
Say "iiii" together.	*Good!*
Story: Use the iguana to tell the story. Emphasize the letter sound.	*Iggy Iguana had an itch. It was a big itch. It was a bad itch. It was a hard to find itch. Imagine that! No matter how he wiggled, he could not find that itch. He scratched his head, but he still itched. He scratched his foot, but he still itched. He rolled over onto his back and inched along, but he still itched. He itched inside and out. Imagine that! _____, do you have an itch?*

Letter Song: Play track #19. Sing along with the "i" song.

Worksheet: Found in the child's workbook on page 21. Show the child how to write the letter "i." Cross out the pictures that *do not* start with the sound of "iiii." Color the pictures that *do* start with the "iiii" sound.

Letter Song: Sing the "i" song again. Repeat the chant of "i" words, pointing to the words and pictures on the next page as you chant.

Final Check: Ask the child: *What letter is this? What does it say? Can you tell me a word that starts with the sound of "iiii"? Good! Now you may keep this little iguana. It will help you remember what "i" says.*

BLENDING: Blend the previous letters together to form words—fix, mix, hit, fib, fit, lid, pit.

Ii

Point to these words as you sing the letter song.

igloo

itch

insect

iguana

Read through the lesson.

LETTER: Zz

PRONUNCIATION: "zzzz" as in zebra

PREPARATION: Punch out Zippy Zebra from the popout letter piece cards.

LETTER REVIEW: Review the previous letters Oo, Xx, and Ii.

ALPHABET SONG: Play track #1. Show the picture flash cards to the child as you sing along with the song.

Zz

LETTER LESSON:

Introduction: Show the child the blue letter card and say:	*This is the letter "z." There is a big "Z" and a small "z." It says "zzzz." What letter is this?*
Point to the card and say "z" together. Ask the child:	*What does it say?*
Say "zzzz" together.	*Good!*
Story: Use the zebra to tell the story. Emphasize the letter sound.	*My name is **Z**ippy **Z**ebra. I live in a very **z**any **z**oo. I like to **z**oom around. Have you ever seen a **z**ebra **z**oom? All the animals in my **z**oo have **z**ip codes on their cages. I love the number **z**ero. My **z**ip code is **00000**. Whenever I go out for a walk, I move in a **z**ig-**z**ag pattern—never in a straight line. My favorite food is **z**ucchini.*

Letter Song: Play track #20. Sing along with the "z" song.

Worksheet: Found in the child's workbook on page 22. Show the child how to write the letter "z." Cross out the pictures that *do not* start with the sound of "zzzz." Color the pictures that *do* start with the "zzzz" sound.

Letter Song: Sing the "z" song again. Repeat the chant of "z" words, pointing to the words and pictures on the next page as you chant.

Final Check: Ask the child:

What letter is this? What does it say? Can you tell me a word that starts with the sound of "zzzz"? Good! Now you may keep this little zebra. It will help you remember what "z" says.

OPTIONAL ACTIVITY: Be Zippy Zebra—zig-zag and zoom around while you are saying "zzzz."

BLENDING: Blend the previous letters together to form words—zig, zag, zip, and zim.

Zz

Point to these words as you sing the letter song.

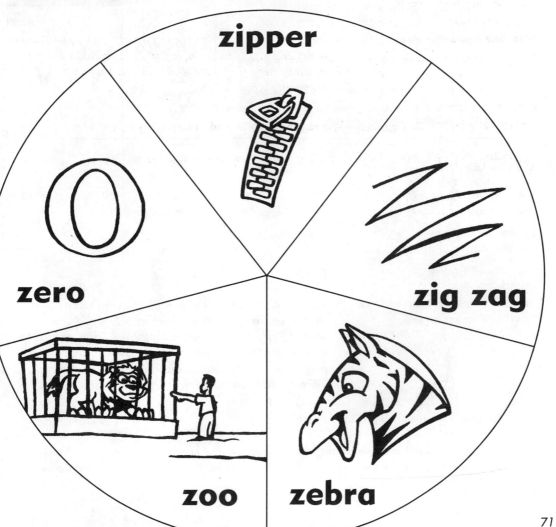

zipper

zig zag

zero

zoo

zebra

71

Read through the lesson.

LETTER: Ww

PRONUNCIATION: "wwww" as in witch

PREPARATION: Punch out Wanda the Witch from the popout letter piece cards.

LETTER REVIEW: Review the previous letters Xx, Ii, and Zz.

ALPHABET SONG: Play track #1. Show the picture flash cards to the child as you sing along with the song.

LETTER LESSON:

Introduction: Show the child the blue letter card and say:	*This is the letter "w." There is a big "W" and a small "w." It says "wwww." What letter is this?*
Point to the card and say "w" together. Ask the child:	*What does it say?*
Say "wwww" together.	*Good!*
Story: Use the witch to tell the story. Emphasize the letter sound.	*Wanda the Witch was watching the children as they wandered through the dark woods. She didn't say a word. She just watched and watched. She wanted to do something wonderful for them. Wanda waved her magic wand.—Whoosh! The darkness disappeared. "Wow!" Said the children. "How beautiful it is!"*

Letter Song: Play track #21. Sing along with the "w" song.

Worksheet: Found in the child's workbook on page 23. Show the child how to write the letter "w." Cross out the pictures that *do not* start with the sound of "wwww." Color the pictures that *do* start with the "wwww" sound.

Letter Song: Sing the "w" song again. Repeat the chant of "w" words, pointing to the words and pictures on the next page as you chant.

Final Check: Ask the child:

What letter is this? What does it say? Can you tell me a word that starts with the sound of "wwww"? Good! Now you may keep this little witch. It will help you remember what "w" says.

OPTIONAL ACTIVITY: Let the witch help you find things around the house that start with "w."

BLENDING: Blend the previous letters together to form words— wax, wig, wag, wit, and win.

Ww

Point to these words as you sing the letter song.

witch

wand

worm

watermelon

Read through the lesson.

LETTERS TO REVIEW: Oo, Xx, Ii, Zz, and Ww.
PREPARATION: Find the letters in the picture flash cards.

REVIEW LESSON:

Introduction: Show the picture flash cards, one letter at a time. Ask the child:

What letter is this? What does it say?

If they are unable to remember, refer to the picture on the card and the story used to teach the letter. Say the letter name and the sound it makes several times.

Worksheet: Show the child the worksheet found in the child's workbook on page 24. Tell them the names of the things pictured, emphasizing the beginning sound. Show them how to match the letter with the picture of the same beginning sound. Draw a line between them with your finger. Then have the child draw the lines with a crayon and color the picture.

Final Check: Show each card again and ask:

What letter is this? What does it say?

Give lots of positive praise and encouragement.

Read through the lesson.

LETTER: Kk

PRONUNCIATION: "kkkk" as in kite

PREPARATION: Punch out Katie the Kite from the popout letter piece cards.

LETTER REVIEW: Review the previous letters Ii, Zz, and Ww.

ALPHABET SONG: Play track #1 Show the picture flash cards to the child as you sing along with the song.

Kk

LETTER LESSON:

Introduction: Show the child the blue letter card and say:	*This is the letter "k." There is a big "K" and a small "k." It says "kkkk." What letter is this?*
Point to the card and say "k" together. Ask the child:	*What does it say?*
Say "kkkk" together.	*Good!*
Story: Use the kite to tell the story. Emphasize the letter sound.	*Katie the Kite flew through the air flipping her tail here and there. She danced over the kids playing in the kindergarten. She sailed over the kittens sitting in the kettle. She swooped past the boys kicking the ball. She flew high past Kangaroo Hill and over the King's palace as she flew in the blue sky. Katie even kissed the sun! Katie loved being a kite!*

Letter Song: Play track #22. Sing along with the "k" song.

Worksheet: Found in the child's workbook on page 25. Show the child how to write the letter "k." Cross out the pictures that *do not* start with the sound of "kkkk." Color the pictures that *do* start with the "kkkk" sound.

Letter Song: Sing the "k" song again. Repeat the chant of "k" words, pointing to the words and pictures on the next page as you chant.

Final Check: Ask the child: *What letter is this? What does it say? Can you tell me a word that starts with the sound of "kkkk"? Good! Now you may keep this little kite. It will help you remember what "k" says.*

OPTIONAL ACTIVITY: Go fly a real kite together and say the "kkkk" sound as you fly it.

BLENDING: Blend the previous letters together to form words—kid, kip, kin, and Kim.

Kk

Point to these words as you sing the letter song.

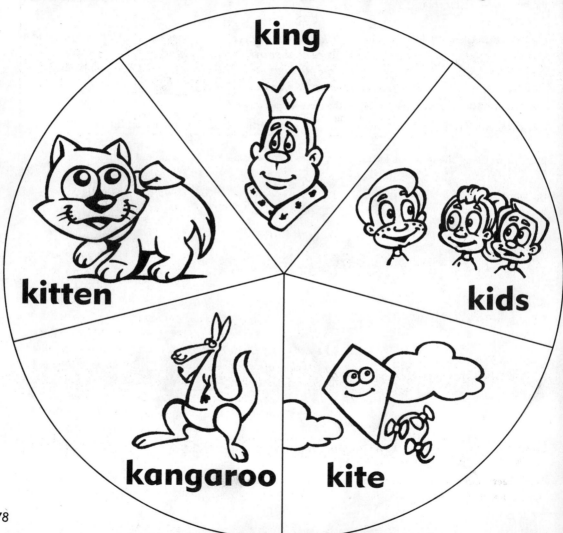

king

kitten

kids

kangaroo

kite

Read through the lesson.

LETTER: Vv

PRONUNCIATION: "vvvv" as in van

PREPRARATION: Punch out Vacation Van from the popout letter piece cards.

LETTER REVIEW: Review the previous letters Zz, Ww, and Kk.

ALPHABET SONG: Play track #1. Show the picture flash cards to the child as you sing along with the song.

LETTER LESSON:

Introduction: Show the child the blue letter card and say:	*This is the letter "v." There is a big "V" and a small "v." It says "vvvv." What letter is this?*
Point to the card and say "v" together. Ask the child:	*What does it say?*
Say "vvvv" together.	*Good!*
Story: Use the van to tell the story. Emphasize the letter sound.	*Val and Vanessa are excited. They are going on a vacation in their van to the village in the valley to visit Aunt Vickie. Val and Vanessa love to help Aunt Vickie. They cook vegetables for supper. They vacuum the floor and pick violets to put in a vase. After supper they put on a program. Val played the violin and Vanessa sang with her beautiful voice. Afterwards, Aunt Vickie served vanilla ice cream. It was a very wonderful vacation*

Letter Song: Play track #23 . Sing along with the "v" song.

Worksheet: Found in the child's workbook on page 26. Show the child how to write the letter "v." Cross out the pictures that *do not* start with the sound of "vvvv." Color the pictures that *do* start with the "vvvv" sound.

Letter Song: Sing the "v" song again. Repeat the chant of "v" words, pointing to the words and pictures on the next page as you chant.

Final Check: Ask the child:

What letter is this? What does it say? Can you tell me a word that starts with the sound of "vvvv"? Good! Now you may keep this little van. It will help you remember what "v" says.

OPTIONAL ACTIVITY: As you drive down the road, look at vans saying "vvvv" every time you see a van.

BLENDING: Blend the previous letters together to form words—van, Val, log, not, kid, and got.

Vv

Point to these words as you sing the letter song.

van

vegetables

violets

violin

Read through the lesson.

LETTER: Uu

PRONUNCIATION: "uuuu" as in umbrella

PREPARATION: Punch out the umbrella from the popout letter piece cards.

LETTER REVIEW: Review the previous letters Ww, Kk, and Vv.

ALPHABET SONG: Play track #1. Show the picture flash cards to the child as you sing along with the song.

Uu

LETTER LESSON:

Introduction: Show the child the blue letter card and say:	*This is the letter "u." There is a big "U" and a small "u." It says "uuuu." What letter is this?*
Point to the card and say "u" together. Ask the child:	*What does it say?*
Say "uuuu" together.	*Good!*
Story: Use the umbrella to tell the story. Emphasize the letter sound.	*Look **up** every body! Look **up**—way **up**! My **uncle** is doing tricks on the wire above **us**. He has an **umbrella** to help him **up** there. He is **unbelievable!!***

Letter Song: Play track #24. Sing along with the "u" song.

Worksheet: Found in the child's workbook on page 27. Show the child how to write the letter "u." Cross out the pictures that *do not* start with the sound of "uuuu". Color the pictures that *do* start with the "uuuu" sound.

Letter Song: Sing the "u" song again. Repeat the chant of "u" words, pointing to the words and pictures on the next page as you chant.

Final Check: Ask the child: *What letter is this? What does it say? Can you tell me a word that starts with the sound of "uuuu"? Good! Now you may keep this little umbrella. It will help you remember what "u" says.*

OPTIONAL ACTIVITY: Find things around the house that start with "u." Take the child for a walk with an umbrella.

BLENDING: Blend the previous letters together to form words—cut, bug, jug, nut, hut, mug, tug, rug.

Uu

Point to these words as you sing the letter song.

uncle

under

umbrella

upside-down

84

LETTER: Ee

PRONUNCIATION: "eeee" as in elephant

PREPARATION: Punch out Elmer the Elephant from the popout letter piece cards.

LETTER REVIEW: Review the previous letters Kk, Vv, and Uu.

ALPHABET SONG: Play track #1. Show the picture flash cards to the child as you sing along with the song.

Ee

LETTER LESSON:

Introduction: Show the child the blue letter card and say:	*This is the letter "e." There is a big "E" and a small "e." It says "eeee." What letter is this?*
Point to the card and say "e" together. Ask the child:	*What does it say?*
Say "eeee" together.	*Good!*
Story: Use the elephant to tell the story. Emphasize the letter sound.	*Elmer the elephant was excited. He was going to the big show on the roof. Everybody was going. Elmer elbowed his way through the entrance and hurried to the elevator. Oh, dear! He didn't quite fit. Everyone pushed on Elmer's back end. "Help!" He cried, his voice echoing. "I don't want to miss the show!" All at once a little elf squeezed his way in and whispered something into Elmer's ear. "What an excellent idea!" Exclaimed Elmer. He made a quick exit and latched onto the elf with his trunk. The escalator was an extra good idea!*

Letter Song: Play track #25. Sing along with the "e" song.

Final Check: Ask the child: *What letter is this? What does it say? Can you tell me a word that starts with the sound of "eeee"? Good! Now you may keep this little elephant. It will help you remember what "e" says.*

OPTIONAL ACTIVITY: Look on billboards for words with "e" in them. Ride on an elevator and an escalator.

BLENDING: Blend the previous letters together to form words—met, get, ten, men, pen, bed, led, and pet.

Ee

Point to these words as you sing the letter song.

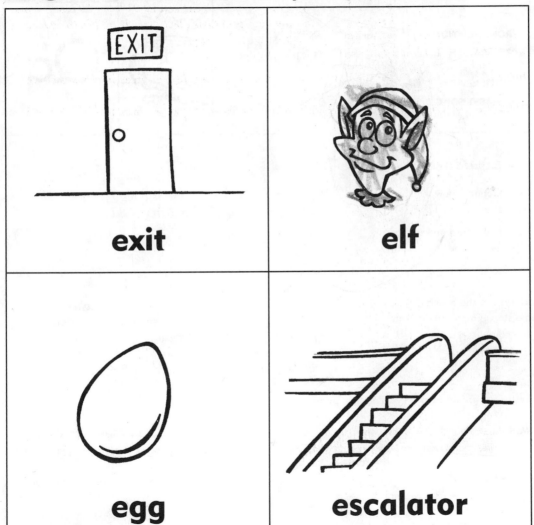

exit

elf

egg

escalator

Read through the lesson.

LETTER: Qq

PRONUNCIATION: "qw" as in queen

PREPARATION: Punch out the queen from the popout letter piece cards.

LETTER REVIEW: Review the previous letters Vv, Uu, and Ee.

ALPHABET SONG: Play track #1. Show the picture flash cards to the child as you sing along with the song.

Qq

LETTER LESSON:

Introduction: Show the child the blue letter card and say:	*This is the letter "q." There is a big "Q" and a small "q." It says "qqqq." What letter is this?*
Point to the card and say "q" together. Ask the child:	*What does it say?*
Say "qqqq" together.	*Good!*
Story: Use the queen to tell the story. Emphasize the letter sound.	*The **q**ueen was **q**uite upset. "Last night when I was snuggled in my **q**uilt, I felt a sudden **q**uake and a **q**uiver. What could it have been?" **q**uestioned the **q**ueen. "Was it an earth**q**uake or was it **Q**uinton the dragon stomping through the kingdom?" What do you think?*

Letter Song: Play track #26. Sing along with the "q" song.

Worksheet: Found in the child's workbook on page 29. Show the child how to write the letter "q." Cross out the pictures that *do not* start with the sound of "qqqq." Color the pictures that *do* start with the "qqqq" sound.

Letter Song: Sing the "q" song again. Repeat the chant of "q" words, pointing to the words and pictures on the next page as you chant.

Final Check: Ask the child:

What letter is this? What does it say? Can you tell me a word that starts with the sound of "qqqq"? Good! Now you may keep this little queen. It will help you remember what "q" says.

OPTIONAL ACTIVITY: Find things around the house that start with "q."

BLENDING: Blend the previous letters together to form words—big, bad, not, hat, hit, and quit.

Qq

Point to these words as you sing the letter song.

quiver

queen

quarter

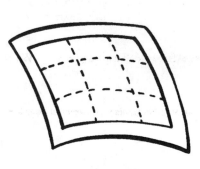

quilt

Read through the lesson.

LETTERS TO REVIEW: Kk, Vv, Uu, Ee, and Qq.

PREPARATION: Find the letters in the picture flash cards.

REVIEW LESSON:

Introduction: Show the picture flash cards, one letter at a time. Ask the child:

What letter is this? What does it say?

If they are unable to remember, refer to the picture on the card and the story used to teach the letter. Say the letter name and the sound it makes several times.

Worksheet: Show the child the worksheet found in the child's workbook on page 30. Tell them the names of the things pictured, emphasizing the beginning sound. Show them how to match the letter with the picture of the same beginning sound. Draw a line between them with your finger. Then have the child draw the lines with a crayon and color the picture.

Final Check: Show each card again and ask:

What letter is this? What does it say?

Give lots of positive praise and encouragement.

Read through the lesson.

LETTER: Yy

PRONUNCIATION: "yyyy" as in yo-yo

PREPARATION: Punch out the yo-yo from the popout letter piece cards.

LETTER REVIEW: Review the previous letters Uu, Ee, and Qq.

ALPHABET SONG: Play track #1. Show the picture flash cards to the child as you sing along with the song.

LETTER LESSON:

Introduction: Show the child the blue letter card and say:	*This is the letter "y." There is a big "Y" and a small "y." It says "yyyy." What letter is this?*
Point to the card and say "y" together. Ask the child:	*What does it say?*
Say "yyyy" together.	*Good!*
Story: Use the yo-yo to tell the story. Emphasize the letter sound.	*Yesterday a young boy was playing in his yard with his yellow yo-yo. The yarn on the yellow yo-yo snapped and the yo-yo spun out of the yard. "Come back!" yelled the boy, but the yo-yo rolled away. The boy yelled to the baker, "Have you seen my yellow yo-yo?" "Yes," he yelled, "it went that way!" The young boy then yelled to the brick layer, "Have you seen my yellow yo-yo?" "Yes, it rolled down the hill!" He called. At the bottom of the hill in a big mud puddle, the young boy found his yucky looking yo-yo. "Oh no, it's not yellow anymore!" he cried. So he washed and shined it all up. "Yes, now my yo-yo is yellow again!"*

Letter Song: Play track #27. Sing along with the "y" song.

Worksheet: Found in the child's workbook on page 31. Show the child how to write the letter "y." Cross out the pictures that *do not* start with the sound of "yyyy." Color the pictures that *do* start with the "yyyy" sound.

Letter Song: Sing the "y" song again. Repeat the chant of "y" words, pointing to the words and pictures on the next page as you chant.

Final Check: Ask the child: *What letter is this? What does it say? Can you tell me a word that starts with the sound of "yyyy"? Good! Now you may keep this little yo-yo. It will help you remember what "y" says.*

OPTIONAL ACTIVITY: Find things around the house that start with "y." Let the child play with a yo-yo.

BLENDING: Blend the previous letters together to form words— yes, yip, yet, and yak.

Yy

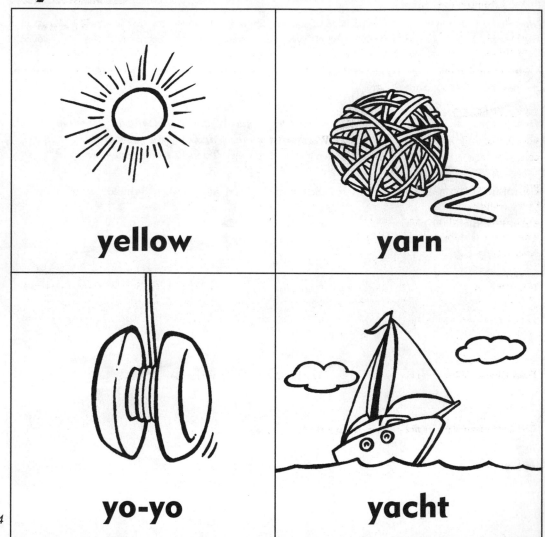

yellow

yarn

yo-yo

yacht

94

Read through the lesson.

LETTERS TO REVIEW: Yy, Ff, Dd, Mm, and Bb.

PREPARATION: Find the letters in the picture flash cards.

REVIEW LESSON:

Introduction: Show the picture flash cards, one letter at a time. Ask the child:

What letter is this? What does it say?

If they are unable to remember, refer to the picture on the card and the story used to teach the letter. Say the letter name and the sound it makes several times.

Worksheet: Show the child the worksheet found in the child's workbook on page 32. Tell them the names of the things pictured, emphasizing the beginning sound. Show them how to match the letter with the picture of the same beginning sound. Draw a line between them with your finger. Then have the child draw the lines with a crayon and color the picture.

Final Check: Show each card again and ask:

What letter is this? What does it say?

Give lots of positive praise and encouragement.

Read through the lesson.

LETTERS: Aa, Ee, Ii, Oo, and Uu.

PRONUNCIATION: At this point we are only using the names of the letters.

PREPARATION: Find both the <u>picture flash cards</u> and the <u>blue letter cards</u>.

ALPHABET SONG: Play track #1. Show the picture flash cards to the child as you sing along with the song.

Identifying Vowels

LETTER LESSON:

Vowels are special letters that have two sounds. The child will be familiar with this because of the alphabet song that is sung every day. Show the child the picture flash cards and say:

Some of the letters have two sounds. Let's see if we can find them.
Does "a" have two sound cards? Yes, I have cards. Say both sounds. Put the blue letter card "a" in front of the child.
Does "b" have two sound cards? No, I have only one card so "b" says only one sound.
Does "t" have two sound cards? No, I have only one card so "t" says only one sound.
Does "d" have two sound cards? No, I have only one card so "d" says only one sound.
Does "e" have two sound cards? Yes, I have two cards. Say both sounds. Put the blue letter card "e" in front of the child.

Continue through the rest of the alphabet until the child has discovered all the vowels and *has the 5 blue cards in front of him*. Say to the child:

These letters are different. They each have two sounds. They are called vowels.

5-Vowel Song: Play the vowel song, track #28. Play it 2 or 3 times and sing along with it .

Worksheet: Do the worksheet on page 33 of the child's workbook.

Final Check: Show the child the 5 vowels on the blue letter cards. Ask the child: *Why are these letters special? (Because they have two sounds.) What are these letters called? (Vowels.)*

Give lots of positive praise and encouragement.

Note: The next 5 lessons will focus on each vowel and its long sound.

LETTER: Aa (long sound)

PRONUNCIATION: "ā" as in angel (the long "ā" says it's own name)

PREPARATION: Punch out Amy Angel from the popout letter piece cards.

5-VOWEL SONG: Play track #28.

Aa

LETTER LESSON:

Introduction: The "a" has two sounds. Show the child both "a" sound cards. Say to the child:

This is the short "a." It makes the "aaaa" sound as in alligator. This is the long "a." It makes the sound "ā" as in angel. It says its own name. Today we will work on the long "ā" sound.

Story: Use the angel to tell the story. Emphasize the letter sound.

Amy Angel was aching all over. She was not even able to sing. "Maybe if I ate some food I would feel better," she thought. Amy Angel put on her apron. She ate some apricot pie. Then she ate some apricot cookies. Then she ate some dried apricots. Amy Angel loves apricots and now she feels much better.

Letter Song: Play track #29. Sing along with the "a" song.

Worksheet: Do the worksheet on page 34 of the child's workbook.

Letter Song: Sing the "a" song again. Repeat the chant of "a" words, pointing to the words and pictures on the next page as you chant.

Final Check: Ask the child:

What letter is this? What are the two sounds that it makes? Good! Now you may keep this angel to help you remember what the long sound of "a" is.

Aa **Point to these words as you sing the letter song.**

angel

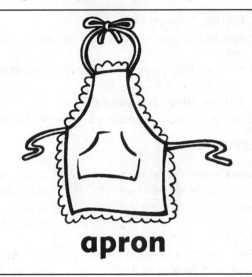

apron

acorn

apricots

LETTER: Ee (long sound)

PRONUNCIATION: "ē" as in eagle (the long "ē" says it's own name)

PREPARATION: Punch out the eagle from the popout letter piece cards.

5-VOWEL SONG: Play track #28.

Ee

LETTER LESSON:

Introduction: The "e" has two sounds. Show the child both "e" sound cards. Say to the child:

This is the short "e." It makes the "eeee" sound as in elephant. This is the long "e." It makes the sound "ē" as in eagle. It says its own name. Today we will work on the long "ē" sound.

Story: Use the eagle to tell the story. Emphasize the letter sound.

The eagle flew high over the mountains. He loved to fly and see all the interesting things below. The eagle saw eleven men eating. He saw eleven slippery eels swimming. He saw eleven artists at their easels. The eagle flew until evening, and then he eased into his nest for the night.

Letter Song: Play track #30. Sing along with the "e" song.

Worksheet: Do the worksheet on page 35 of the child's workbook.

Letter Song: Sing the "e" song again. Repeat the chant of "e" words, pointing to the words and pictures on the next page as you chant.

Final Check: Ask the child:

What letter is this? What are the two sounds that it makes? Good! Now you may keep this eagle to help you remember what the long sound of "e" is.

Ee

Point to these words as you sing the letter song.

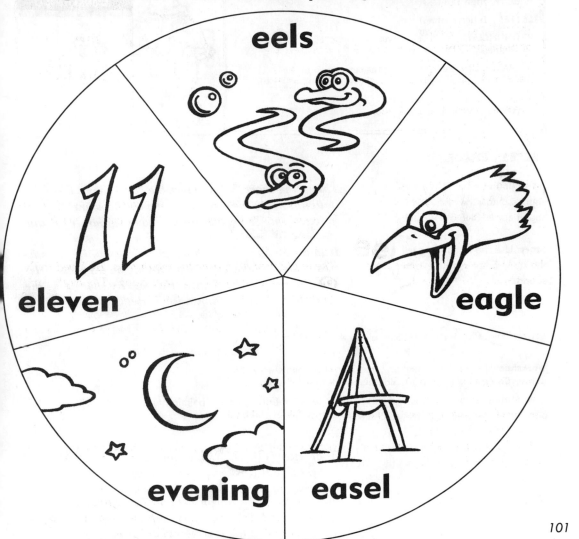

eels

eagle

eleven

evening

easel

Read through the lesson.

LETTER: Ii (long sound)

PRONUNCIATION: "ī" as in Ivan (the long "ī" says it's own name)

PREPARATION: Punch out Ivan the penguin from the popout letter piece cards.

5-VOWEL SONG: Play track #28.

Ii

LETTER LESSON:

Introduction: The "i" has two sounds. Show the child both "i" sound cards. Say to the child:

This is the short "i." It makes the "iiii" sound as in indian. This is the long "i." It makes the sound "ī" as in ice cream. Today we will work on the long "ī" sound.

Story: Use the penguin to tell the story. Emphasize the letter sound.

Ivan the Penguin loves things that are cold. He loves ice cream cones. He loves icicles hanging on the house. He loves ice cubes in his punch. He loves ice skating on the pond. Ivan even lives in an ice house.

Letter Song: Play track #31. Sing along with the "i" song.

Worksheet: Do the worksheet on page 36 of the child's workbook.

Letter Song: Sing the "i" song again. Repeat the chant of "i" words, pointing to the words and pictures on the next page as you chant.

Final Check: Ask the child:

What letter is this? What are the two sounds that it makes? Good! Now you may keep Ivan the Penguin to help you remember what the long sound of "i" is.

Ii

Point to these words as you sing the letter song.

ice cream

island

ivy

icicles

Read through the lesson.

LETTER: Oo (long sound)

PRONUNCIATION: "ō" as in oatmeal (the long "ō" says it's own name)

PREPARATION: Punch out Olga in overall eating oatmeal from the popout letter piece cards.

5-VOWEL SONG: Play track #28.

Oo

LETTER LESSON:

Introduction: The "o" has two sounds. Show the child both "o" sound cards. Say to the child:

This is the short "o." It makes the "oooo" sound as in octopus. This is the long "o." It makes the sound "ō" as in oatmeal. Today we will work on the long "ō" sound.

Story: Use Olga to tell the story. Emphasize the letter sound.

Olga put on her overalls and her old overcoat and went for a walk by the ocean. It was only a short walk because the wind was cold as it blew in over the waves. When she got home, she took off her overcoat and ate a warm bowl of oatmeal for breakfast.

Letter Song: Play track #32. Sing along with the "o" song.

Worksheet: Do the worksheet on page 37 of the child's workbook.

Letter Song: Sing the "o" song again. Repeat the chant of "o" words, pointing to the words and pictures on the next page as you chant.

Final Check: Ask the child:

What letter is this? What are the two sounds that it makes? Good! Now you may keep Olga to help you remember what the long sound of "o" is.

Oo

oatmeal

overalls

ogre

overcoat

Lesson 38

Uu

LETTER: Uu (long sound)

PRONUNCIATION: "ū" as in unicorn (the long "ū" says it's own name)

PREPARATION: Punch out Uni the Unicorn from the popout letter piece cards.

5-VOWEL SONG: Play track #28.

LETTER LESSON:

Introduction: The "u" has two sounds. Show the child both "u" sound cards. Say to the child:

This is the short "u." It makes the "uuuu" sound as in umbrella. This is the long "u." It makes the sound "ū" as in unicorn. Today we will work on the long "ū" sound.

Story: Use the unicorn to tell the story. Emphasize the letter sound.

*Uni the Unicorn was having so much fun riding his **u**nicycle. Next he played his **u**ke and tried on his dad's **u**niform. **U**ni the Unicorn loves days like this!*

Letter Song: Play track #33 . Sing along with the "u" song.

Worksheet: Do the worksheet on page 38 of the child's workbook.

Letter Song: Sing the "u" song again. Repeat the chant of "u" words, pointing to the words and pictures on the next page as you chant.

Final Check: Ask the child:

What letter is this? What are the two sounds that it makes? Good! Now you may keep this unicorn to help you remember what the long sound of "u" is.

Uu

Point to these words as you sing the letter song.

unicorn

uniform

United States

unicycle

Read through the lesson.

LETTERS: Aa, Ee, Ii, Oo, and Uu.

PRONUNCIATION: Long vowel sounds. The letters say their own names.

PREPARATION: Find the blue letter cards for the vowels. Have paper or a chalk board to write on.

5-VOWEL SONG: Play track #28.

Using Vowels

LETTER LESSON:

Introduction: Ask the child:

What are the vowels? (Aa, Ee, Ii, Oo and Uu.) How many sounds do they have? (two)

Display the blue card as they say the vowel.

5-Vowel Song: Play the vowel song, track #28.   Sing along with the song.

Say to the child:

Vowels are important because all words have vowels in them.

Write some words for the child and have them pick out the vowels (sad, pet, pig, mom, bug). Have them pick out the vowels in their own name.

Worksheet: Do worksheets on pages 39-44 of the child's workbook. Have the child write in the vowels.

Final Check: Ask the child:

What letters are vowels? (a, e, i, o, u) Why are they important? (Because they are in all words.)

Review the vowels and sing the vowel song for the next few days. Each time you do, have the child do one or two vowel worksheets until all six vowel worksheets, page numbers 39 thru 44, are completed. Make sure the child has a good understanding of the vowels before going on to the two-vowel lesson and two-vowel reading books.

Read through the lesson.

LETTERS: Aa, Ee, Ii, Oo, and Uu

PRONUNCIATION: When there are two vowels in a word, the first vowel says its long sound (it says its own name) and the second vowel is silent.

PREPARATION: Display the blue letter cards of the vowels. Have paper available to write on.

TWO-VOWEL RULE SONG: Play track #34.

LETTER LESSON:

Introduction: Say to the child:

Sometimes we have words with two vowels in them. This is the rule: When two vowels go walking, the first one does the talking, and it says its own name. The second vowel goes to sleep.

Repeat the rule.

Two-Vowel Rule Song: Play the two-vowel song, track #34. Listen to the song and sing along with it. You may want to play it again.

Write a word that has two vowels together (rain). Have the child cross out the second vowel and put the long mark over the first vowel (rāin). The long mark reminds them that the "a" says its own name when the second vowel is asleep. Then have the child sound out the word using the rule you just taught them.

Write more words and do the same thing—bead, goat, coat, feet, and bee.

Two-Vowel Rule Song: Play the two-vowel song again. Listen to the song and sing along with it. You may want to play it again.

Worksheet: Do the worksheets on pages 45 and 46 of the child's workbook.

Final Check: Ask the child:

What letters are vowels? When there are two vowels in a word, what does the first one say? What does the second vowel do?

Read through the lesson.

LETTER: Aa, Ee, Ii, Oo, and Uu

PRONUNCIATION: Say the letter names.

PREPARATION: Find the blue letter cards a, e, i, o and u.

TWO-VOWEL RULE SONG: Play track #34.

LETTER LESSON:

Introduction: Review the two-vowel rule. Say to the child:

When two vowels go walking, the first one does the talking, and it says its own name. The second vowel goes to sleep.

Two-Vowel Rule Song: Play the two-vowel song, track #34. Listen to the song and sing along with it. You may want to play it again.

Say to the child:

When two vowels are in a word, they are not always together. Sometimes they have another letter in between them, but the rule is still the same. The first vowel says its own name or long sound and the second vowel is silent. Write words that follow this rule (cape, bite, made, kite, cake, rope). When you write the word, have the child put the long mark over the first vowel, cross out the second vowel, and sound out the word—cape.

Worksheet: There are seven worksheets practicing two-vowel rules, page numbers 47 to 53 of the child's workbook. You can repeat this lesson 2-3 times until all the worksheets are done and the child really understands this concept.

Lesson Manual 2

Read through the lesson.

R BLENDS

CONSONANT BLEND: Two consonants that are blended together and make one sound.

PRONUNCIATION: Pronunciation varies depending on each letter in the consonant blend. Here are the "r" blend sounds we are going to learn:

br - as in <u>br</u>own	**fr** - as in <u>fr</u>esh <u>fr</u>uit	**pr** - as in <u>pr</u>ize
cr - as in <u>cr</u>ayon	**gr** - as in <u>gr</u>een	**tr** - as in <u>tr</u>ee
dr - as in <u>dr</u>op	**kr** - as in <u>Kr</u>is	

r
Blends

BLEND LESSON:

Introduction: Show the child the first blend card and say:	*When we say these two letters together, they make one sound.*
Point to the first letter in the blend.	*What letter is this? What sound does it make?*
Point to the second letter in the blend.	*What letter is this? What sound does it make?*
Point to the blend and say the two letters together. Ask the child: Repeat these steps for each blend card.	*What do these two letters say together?*
Story: Read this story while the child listens for the blend sounds. Be sure to emphasize the blends so that the child can recognize them.	***Brad*** *likes to* ***draw. Brad draws brown trees*** *and* ***green grass. Brad*** *also* ***draws bright fruit. Brad draws*** *with his new* ***crayons. Brad's drawings*** *are* ***great. Brad*** *even won a* ***grand prize*** *for one of his best* ***drawings.*** *Brad loves to* ***draw*** *with his* ***crayons.***
Blend Review: Hold up each flash card, then ask the child:	*What does this say? Can you tell me a word that starts with this sound?*

Practice: Have the child read the "r" blend words on the backs of the flash cards. Practice these words. They will be used in the books you read with this lesson.

brown*, Brad, broom*, crack, crayons*, creep, dress, drag, drop, Fred, fruit, from*, grab, Gram, grass, gray, green, Kris, Prim, prize, prop, tree, tries, trip, and trunk

*sight word.

Read the books <u>Miss Prim</u> and <u>The Green Crayon</u> (Books 34 & 35)

OPTIONAL ACTIVITY: Read the story again. This time, have the child lay the flash cards out on the table. As you read the words, have the child point to the correct blend.

Lesson 2

S BLENDS

CONSONANT BLEND: Two consonants that are blended together and make one sound.

PRONUNCIATION: Pronunciation varies depending on each letter in the consonant blend. Here are the "s" blend sounds we are going to learn:

sk - as in <u>sk</u>ate   **sn** - as in <u>sn</u>ap   **sl** - as in <u>sl</u>ide
sp - as in <u>sp</u>ider   **sm** - as in <u>sm</u>ell   **st** - as in <u>st</u>ick

S Blends

BLEND LESSON:

Introduction: Show the child the first blend card and say:	*When we say these two letters together, they make one sound.*
Point to the first letter in the blend.	*What letter is this? What sound does it make?*
Point to the second letter in the blend.	*What letter is this? What sound does it make?*
Point to the blend and say the two letters together. Ask the child: Repeat these steps for each blend card.	*What do these two letters say together?*
Story: Read this story while the child listens for the blend sounds. Be sure to emphasize the blends so that the child can recognize them.	**Skip** loves **snakes** and **snails** and **spiders**. **Skip** likes to play with the **slithery**, **slim**y animals. **Skip** likes the **skin** on a **snake**. His hands **slide** on the **smooth skin**. **Skip** likes to **skate** through the park and look under **sticks** for **snails** and **spiders**. **Skip** hopes he doesn't find a **skunk**. No one likes the **smell** of a **skunk**.
Blend Review: Hold up each flash card, then ask the child:	*What does this say? Can you tell me a word that starts with this sound?*

Practice: Have the child read the "s" blend words on the backs of the flash cards. Practice these words. They will be used in the books you read with this lesson.

skate, skin, skunk, slam, slide, slimy*, slip, slither*, smell, small*, smack, snap, snakes, snails, spiders*, spin, spun, stink, Stan, stick

*sight word.

Read the books <u>Smile</u> and <u>Snakes and Snails</u> (Books 36 & 37)

OPTIONAL ACTIVITY: Read the story again. This time, have the child lay the flash cards out on the table. As you read the words, have the child point to the correct blend.

Read through the lesson.

L BLENDS

CONSONANT BLEND: Two consonants that are blended together and make one sound.

PRONUNCIATION: Pronunciation varies depending on each letter in the consonant blend. Here are the "l" blend sounds we are going to learn:

bl - as in <u>bl</u>ue   **cl** - as in <u>cl</u>ock   **fl** - as in <u>fl</u>ip
gl - as in <u>gl</u>ue   **pl** - as in <u>pl</u>ane   **sl** - as in <u>sl</u>eep

l

Blends

BLEND LESSON:

Introduction: Show the child the first blend card and say:	*When we say these two letters together, they make one sound.*
Point to the first letter in the blend.	*What letter is this? What sound does it make?*
Point to the second letter in the blend.	*What letter is this? What sound does it make?*
Point to the blend and say the two letters together. Ask the child: Repeat these steps for each blend card.	*What do these two letters say together?*
Story: Read this story while the child listens for the blend sounds. Be sure to emphasize the blends so that the child can recognize them.	***Blake plays*** *with* ***blue blocks. Blake*** *builds a* ***clock. Blake*** *builds a* ***blue plane. Blake*** *does not have* ***black blocks,*** *just* ***flat, blue blocks. Blake plays*** *with his* ***blue blocks*** *all day.* ***Blake*** *keeps his* ***blue blocks clean. Blake*** *likes to* ***play*** *with* ***blue blocks.***
Blend Review: Hold up each flash card, then ask the child:	*What does this say? Can you tell me a word that starts with this sound?*

Practice: Have the child read the "l" blend words on the backs of the flash cards. Practice these words. They will be used in the books you read with this lesson.

black, Blake, blue, clean, clue, clock, Flip, Flop, fleas, Glen, glad, glue, plane, plan, plum, sleep, slip, slide

Read the books <u>Flip and Flop</u> and <u>The Blue Plane</u> (Books 38 & 39)

OPTIONAL ACTIVITY: Read the story again. This time, have the child lay the flash cards out on the table. As you read the words, have the child point to the correct blend.

Read through the lesson.

str
scr

THREE LETTER BLENDS: str, scr

CONSONANT BLEND: Three consonants that are blended together and make one sound.

PRONUNCIATION: **str** - as in <u>str</u>aw, <u>str</u>ing, and <u>str</u>eam
                              scr - as in <u>scr</u>eam, <u>scr</u>ape, and <u>scr</u>atch

BLEND LESSON:

Introduction: Show the child the first blend card and say:	*When we say these three letters together, they make one sound.*
Point to the first letter in the blend.	*What letter is this? What sound does it make?*
Point to the second letter in the blend.	*What letter is this? What sound does it make?*
Point to the third letter in the blend.	*What letter is this? What sound does it make?*
Point to the blend and say the three letters together. Ask the child: Repeat these steps for each blend card.	*What do these three letters say together?*
Story: Read this story while the child listens for the blend sounds. Be sure to emphasize the blends so that the child can recognize them.	***Scruff*** *is a **strong** dog. **Scruff** runs and his paws **scrape** the **street**. When **Scruff** sees other dogs, he **struts** and **stretches** his legs. **Scruff** knows he is the **strongest**. One day, **Scruff** heard a boy **scream**. **Scruff** ran down the **street** and found the boy. He was hurt. He had a big **scratch**. **Scruff** carried the boy down the **street** to his home. **Scruff** saved the day.*
Blend Review: Hold up each flash card, then ask the child:	*What does this say? Can you tell me a word that starts with this sound?*

Practice: Have the child read the 3-letter blend words on the backs of the flash cards. Practice these words. They will be used in the books you read with this lesson.

street, strut, stripe, scrape, Scruff, scream

While teaching this lesson and the next two lessons, you should start reading the following books: <u>The Big Parade</u>, <u>The Pink Cast</u>, <u>The Fair</u>, and <u>Gwen</u> (Books 40, 41, 42, & 43). These books all focus on the three consonant blends taught in lessons 4, 5, and 6.

OPTIONAL ACTIVITY: Read the story again. This time, have the child lay the flash cards out on the table. As you read the words, have the child point to the correct blend.

Read through the lesson.

THREE LETTER BLENDS: spl, spr

CONSONANT BLEND: Three consonants that are blended together and make one sound.

PRONUNCIATION: **spl** - as in <u>spl</u>it and <u>spl</u>ash
　　　　　　　spr - as in <u>spr</u>ay and <u>spr</u>ing

spl
spr

BLEND LESSON:

Introduction: Show the child the first blend card and say:	*When we say these three letters together, they make one sound.*
Point to the first letter in the blend.	*What letter is this? What sound does it make?*
Point to the second letter in the blend.	*What letter is this? What sound does it make?*
Point to the third letter in the blend.	*What letter is this? What sound does it make?*
Point to the blend and say the three letters together. Ask the child:	*What do these three letters say together?*
Repeat these steps for each blend card.	
Story: Read this story while the child listens for the blend sounds. Be sure to emphasize the blends so that the child can recognize them.	***Spring** is a great time. Flowers are **sprouting**. Kids **splish** and **splash** in the pool. Kids **spray** their friends to keep cool. Some kids **sprint** around a track. Lucky kids eat banana **splits**. Everyone has fun in the **Spring**.*
Blend Review: Hold up each flash card, then ask the child:	*What does this say? Can you tell me a word that starts with this sound?*

Practice: Have the child read the 3-letter blend words on the backs of the flash cards. Practice these words. They will be used in the books you read with this lesson.

splish*, splash*, split, spray*, sprint, sprain

*sight word.

While teaching this lesson you should start reading the following books: <u>The Big Parade</u>, <u>The Pink Cast</u>, <u>The Fair</u>, and <u>Gwen</u> (Books 40, 41, 42, & 43). These books all focus on the three consonant blends taught in lessons 4, 5, and 6.

OPTIONAL ACTIVITY: Read the story again. This time, have the child lay the flash cards out on the table. As you read the words, have the child point to the correct blend.

Read through the lesson.

THREE LETTER BLEND: squ

CONSONANT BLEND: Three consonants that are blended together and make one sound.

PRONUNCIATION: squ - as in s<u>qu</u>eak and s<u>qu</u>are

BLEND LESSON:

Introduction: Show the child the blend card and say:	*When we say these three letters together, they make one sound.*
Point to the first letter in the blend.	*What letter is this? What sound does it make?*
Point to the second letter in the blend.	*What letter is this? What sound does it make?*
Point to the third letter in the blend.	*What letter is this? What sound does it make?*
Point to the blend and say the three letters together. Ask the child:	*What do these three letters say together?*
Story: Read this story while the child listens for the blend sounds. Be sure to emphasize the blends so that the child can recognize them.	*A man named **Squire** has a **square** door. This **square** door **squeaks** all the time. **Squire** is tired of the **squeak**. **Squire** tries everything. **Squire** put a **squid** on the **square** door. Silly **Squire**, **squid** will not stop a **squeak**. **Squire squirts** oil on the **square** door. The **squeak** stops. **Squire** is glad the **squeak** is gone.*
Blend Review: Hold up each flash card, then ask the child:	*What does this say? Can you tell me a word that starts with this sound?*

Practice: Have the child read the 3-letter blend words on the back of the flash card. Practice these words. They will be used in the books you read with this lesson.

squeak, squeal, square, squid

While teaching this lesson you should finish reading the following books: <u>The Big Parade</u>, <u>The Pink Cast</u>, <u>The Fair</u>, and <u>Gwen</u> (Books 40, 41, 42, & 43). These books all focus on the three consonant blends taught in lessons 4, 5, and 6.

OPTIONAL ACTIVITY: Read the story again. This time, have the child lay the flash cards out on the table. As you read the words, have the child point to the correct blend.

Read through the lesson.

BLENDS TO REVIEW: r blends, s blends, l blends, str, scr, spl, spr, squ

PREPARATION: Get out the flash card for each blend.

REVIEW LESSON:

Introduction: Show the flash cards one at a time. Ask the child:

What sound do these letters make?

If they are unable to remember, ask the child what each letter is and what sound it makes (just as you did in the lessons). Then ask what sound the two or three letters make when you say them together.

Give lots of positive praise and encouragement.

Read through the lesson.

DIGRAPH: sh

CONSONANT DIGRAPH: Two consonants that are blended together and make one sound.

PRONUNCIATION: **"shhh"** - as in <u>sh</u>arp and fi<u>sh</u>
The sh digraph makes the same sound no matter where it is found in a word.

sh

DIGRAPH LESSON:

Introduction: Show the flash card and say:	*When we say these two letters together, they make one sound.*
Point to the "s" and ask:	*What letter is this? What sound does it make?*
Point to the "h" and ask:	*What letter is this? What sound does it make?*
Point to the digraph and say:	*"s" and "h" make the "shhhhh" sound when they are together.*
Point to the card again and ask the child:	*What sound does this make?*
Story: Read this story while the child listens for the digraph sounds. Be sure to emphasize the digraphs so that the child can recognize them.	***Shannon** loves the sea **shore**. **She** collects **shells** and looks for **fish**. **Shannon** even saw a **shark** once. **Shannon** also takes her dog, **Shep** to the sea **shore**. **Shep** has a **leash** so he doesn't run away. The sun **shines** and **shines** at the sea **shore**. **Shannon** loves to go to the sea **shore**.*
Digraph Review: Hold up the flash card, then ask the child:	*What sound does this make? Can you tell me a word that starts with this sound?*

Practice: Have the child read the diagraph words on the back of the flash card. Practice these words. They will be used in the books you read with this lesson.

Shane, shin, shine, Josh, wish, trash

Read <u>Shane Finds His Smile</u>, and <u>Josh Can Help</u> (Books 44 & 45).

OPTIONAL ACTIVITY: Read the story again. This time, have the child hold up the flash card each time you read a word with the sh digraph.

Read through the lesson.

DIGRAPH: th

CONSONANT DIGRAPH: Two consonants that are blended together and make one sound.

PRONUNCIATION: **"thhh"** - breathy as in <u>th</u>umb and ma<u>th</u>
                                    "thh" - harder as in <u>th</u>ey, <u>th</u>e, or <u>th</u>em

th

DIGRAPH LESSON:

Introduction: Show the flash card and say:	*When we say these two letters together, they make one sound.*
Point to the "t" and ask:	*What letter is this? What sound does it make?*
Point to the "h" and ask:	*What letter is this? What sound does it make?*
Point to the digraph and say:	*The "t" and the "h" make a "thhhh" sound when they are together. Sometimes it is like "thhh" in thumb. Other times it sounds like "thh" in they and them.*
Point to the card again and ask the child:	*What sound does this make?*

Be sure to help your child recognize the two different sounds the "th" digraph makes. You may have to simply have your child memorize words like they and them that uses the harder "th" sound. Remember, "th" only makes the harder sound at the beginning of words, never at the end.

Story: Read this story while the child listens for the digraph sounds. Be sure to emphasize the diagraphs so that the child can recognize them.

Thad has thick thumbs. Thad's thumbs are always getting stuck. Thad's thumbs will not fit in a thimble. They are just too big. Even though Thad has thick thumbs, he would never trade them for thin thumbs. Thad thinks thick is better.

Digraph Review: Hold up the flash card, then ask the child:

What sound does this make? Can you tell me a word that starts with this sound?

Practice: Have the child read the digraph words on the back of the flash card. Practice these words. They will be used in the books you read with this lesson.

Thad, thick, thin, Seth, Beth, sloth

Read <u>Thad Toad</u>, and <u>Seth and Beth</u> (Books 46 & 47).

OPTIONAL ACTIVITY: Read the story again. This time, have the child hold up the flash card each time you read a word with the th digraph.

Read through the lesson.

DIGRAPH: ch

CONSONANT DIGRAPH: Two consonants that are blended together and make one sound.

PRONUNCIATION: "ch" - as in <u>ch</u>eese and lun<u>ch</u>
The "ch" digraph makes the same sound no matter where it is found in a word.

ch

DIGRAPH LESSON:

Introduction: Show the flash card and say:	*When we say these two letters together, they make one sound.*
Point to the "c" and ask:	*What letter is this? What sound does it make?*
Point to the "h" and ask:	*What letter is this? What sound does it make?*
Point to the digraph and say:	*"c" and "h" make the "ch" sound when they are together.*
Point to the card again and ask the child:	*What sound does this make?*
Story: Read this story while the child listens for the digraph sounds. Be sure to emphasize the digraphs so that the child can recognize them.	***Chuck chomps** on **cheese** all day long. **Chuck** has **cheese** for **lunch**. **Chuck** just likes to **munch** his **cheese**. Sometimes **Chuck** gets **cheese** on his **chin** or **cheese** on his **cheek**. **Chuck** is so busy **munching** that he doesn't even care. **Chuck chomps** on **cheese** all day long. **Chuck** is a mouse.*
Digraph Review: Hold up the flash card, then ask the child:	*What sound does this make? Can you tell me a word that starts with this sound?*

Practice: Have the child read the digraph words on the back of the flash card. Practice these words. They will be used in the books you read with this lesson.

Chad, champ, cheer, lunch, munch, peach

Read <u>Chad and Ben</u>, and <u>Mitch and the Peach</u> (Books 48 & 49).

OPTIONAL ACTIVITY: Read the story again. This time, have the child hold up the flash card each time you read a word with the ch digraph.

Read through the lesson.

DIGRAPH: wh

CONSONANT DIGRAPH: Two consonants that are blended together and make one sound.

PRONUNCIATION: **"whhh"** - very breathy as in wh_ale and wh_istle

wh

DIGRAPH LESSON:

Introduction: Show the flash card and say:	*When we say these two letters together, they make one sound.*
Point to the "w" and ask:	*What letter is this? What sound does it make?*
Point to the "h" and ask:	*What letter is this? What sound does it make?*
Point to the digraph and say:	*"w" and "h" make the "whhhhh" sound when they are together. (Puff your cheeks and blow air to exaggerate the "wh" sound.)*
Point to the card again and ask the child:	*What sound does this make?*
Story: Read this story while the child listens for the digraph sounds. Be sure to emphasize the digraphs so that the child can recognize them.	***White whales whistle while** they swim. **Whales whistle wherever** they go. **Whistling** is fun. These **white whales whistle when** they are happy. Can you **whistle** like the **white whale?** **Why** don't you try it?*
Digraph Review: Hold up the flash card, then ask the child:	*What sound does this make? Can you tell me a word that starts with this sound?*

Practice: Have the child read the digraph words on the back of the flash card. Practice these words. They will be used in the books you read with this lesson.

whale, when, where*, white, why*

*sight words

Read <u>Why?</u>, and <u>Trip to Sea</u> (Books 50 & 51).

OPTIONAL ACTIVITY: Read the story again. This time, have the child hold up the flash card each time you read a word with the wh digraph.

Read through the lesson.

SOFT C RULE: When the letter "c" is followed by either an "i" or an "e", it makes the sound of "sss".

PRONUNCIATION: **"sss"** - as in rice, nice, and slice

SOFT "C" LESSON:

Introduction: Show the flash card and say:	*When there is an "i" or an "e" after a "c" it changes the "c" sound to "sss".*
Clap a rythm and chant this rule several times with the child:	*An i or an e after a c changes the "c" to "sss".*
Point to the card and say:	*"c" and "e" make the "sss" sound when they are together.*
Point to the card again and ask the child:	*What sound does this make?*
Story: Read this story while the child listens for the soft "c." Be sure to emphasize the soft "c" so that the child can recognize it.	***Mice** play **dice**. **Mice** eat **rice**. **Mice** wrap **lace** around their **face**. **Mice race** back to their **place**. These **mice** are **nice**. They share **rice**. They share **dice**. They even share a **slice** of pie. These **mice** are **nice**.*
Soft c Review: Hold up the flashcard, then ask the child:	*What sound does this make? Can you tell me a word that has this sound?*

Practice: Have the child read the soft "c" words on the back of the flash card. Practice these words. They will be used in the books you read with this lesson.

mice, race, nice, slice, and ice.

Read <u>The Race</u> (Book 52).

OPTIONAL ACTIVITY: Read the story again. This time, have the child hold up the flash card each time you read a word with the soft "c" sound.

SOFT G RULE: When the letter g is followed by either an i or an e, it makes the sound of "j".
PRONUNCIATION: **"j"** - as in g̲iant, hug̲e, ag̲e

SOFT "G" LESSON:

Introduction: Show the flash card and say:	*When there is an "i" or an "e" after a "g" it changes the "g" sound to "j".*
Clap a rythm and chant this rule several times with the child:	*An "i" or an "e" after a "g" changes the "g" to "j".*
Point to the card and say:	*"g" and "e" make the "j" sound when they are together.*
Point to the card again and ask the child:	*What sound does this make?*
Story: Read this story while the child listens for the soft "g." Be sure to emphasize the soft "g" so that the child can recognize it.	*The **gentle giant** is **huge**. Some people are scared because he is so **huge**. They want to put him in a **cage**. But the **gentle giant** is **gentle**, not mean. He should not be in a **cage**. **Gene** knows the **gentle giant**. **Gene** knows that the **giant** is **huge**, but not mean. **Gene** is not scared. **Gene** will not let them put the **gentle giant** in a **cage**. The **gentle giant** is **Gene's** friend.*
Soft g Review: Hold up the flash card, then ask the child:	*What sound does this make? Can you tell me a word that has this sound?*

Practice: Have the child read the soft "g" words on the back of the flash card. Practice these words. They will be used in the books you read with this lesson.

Gene, huge, cage, edge*

*sight word

Read <u>Huge Gene</u> (Book 53).

OPTIONAL ACTIVITY: Read the story again. This time, have the child hold up the flash card each time you read a word with the soft "g" sound.

Read through the lesson.

REVIEW: sh, th, ch, wh, soft c, and soft g

PREPARATION: Get out the flash card for each blend.

REVIEW LESSON:

Introduction: Show the flash cards one at a time. Ask the child:

What sound do these letters make?

If the child is unable to remember, turn back to the lesson they are having trouble with. Go though the introduction section again, then try reviewing. If they are still having difficulty, it may be best to wait a few days then repeat the lesson.

Give lots of positive praise and encouragement.